WITHDRAWN
UTSA LIBRARIES

Recognitions in
Gestalt Therapy

Recognitions in
Gestalt Therapy

SELECTED BY

Paul David Pursglove

FUNK & WAGNALLS · New York

Copyright © 1968 by Paul David Pursglove
All Rights Reserved.
Library of Congress Catalog Card Number: 68-29123
Published by Funk & Wagnalls, *A Division of* Reader's Digest Books,
Inc.

"Golden Age" by Paul Goodman originally appeared in *Complex*.
Copyright 1953 by The 5 x 8 Press.

"Growing Up" by Paul Goodman originally appeared in *Five Years*
(Brussel & Brussel). Copyright © 1966 by Paul Goodman. All Rights
Reserved.

"Human Nature and the Anthropology of Neurosis" by Paul Goodman appears in *Gestalt Therapy* (Julian Press, Inc.). Copyright 1950
by Arts & Science Press, Copyright 1951 by Frederick Perls, M.D.,
Ph.D., Ralph F. Hefferline, Ph.D., and Paul Goodman, Ph.D.

"A Syllabus of Psychotherapy" by Paul Goodman appears in *Empire
City* (The Macmillan Company, 1964). Copyright © 1959 by Paul
Goodman. All Rights Reserved.

"Experiential Family Therapy" by Walter Kempler, M.D., originally
appeared in *The International Journal of Group Psychotherapy*.
Copyright 1965, American Group Psychotherapy Association, Inc.

"Notes on the Psychology of Give and Take" by Dr. Laura Perls
originally appeared in *Complex*. Copyright 1953 by The 5 x 8 Press.

"Two Instances of Gestalt Therapy" by Dr. Laura Perls originally
appeared in *Case Reports in Clinical Psychology*. Copyright © 1956
by The Department of Psychology, Kings County Hospital, Brook-
lyn 3, New York. All Rights Reserved.

"A Contemporary Psychotherapy" by Erving Polster originally appeared in *Psychotherapy: Theory, Research and Practice*. Copyright
1966 by Psychologists Interested in the Advancement of Psychotherapy. All Rights Reserved.

"Movement Therapy" by Joseph Schlichter appears for the first time
in this volume. Copyright © 1968 by Joseph Schlichter. All Rights
Reserved.

"Existential Analytic Psychotherapy" by Dr. Wilson Van Dusen
originally appeared in *The American Journal of Psychoanalysis*.
Copyright 1960 by The Association for the Advancement of Psychoanalysis.

Printed in the United States of America

The Professor himself is uncanonical enough; he is beating with his hand, with his fist, on the headpiece of the old-fashioned horsehair sofa that had heard more secrets than the confession box of any popular Roman Catholic father-confessor in his heyday. This was the homely historical instrument of the original scheme of psychotherapy, of psychoanalysis, the science of the unravelling of the tangled skeins of the unconscious mind and the healing implicit in the process. *Consciously,* I was not aware of having said anything that might account for the professor's outburst. And even as I veered around facing him, my mind was detached enough to wonder if this was some idea of *his* for speeding up the analytic content or redirecting the flow of associated images. The Professor said, "The trouble is—I am an old man—you do not think it worth your while to love me."

—from *Tribute to Freud* by the poet
H. D. (New York: Pantheon, 1956)

Editor's Note

In this collection of writings by Gestalt psychotherapists and others, like Dr. Van Dusen, who are friendly to the Gestalt approach, there is nowhere a complete and explicit statement either of what a Gestalt is or of what Gestalt Therapy "is." You can find the noun Gestalt in a dictionary. But only the *experience* of Gestalt Therapy could provide you with a means for saying what it "is." In my own experience as patient and therapist I have found it less and less necessary to define and draw verbal borders "about" therapy. This relieves and refreshes me. But if you need thorough technical and theoretical satisfaction, please read *Gestalt Therapy* by Frederick S. Perls, Ralph Hefferline, and Paul Goodman.* Also, see the Bibliography in this book (147–149).

* New York: Julian Press, 1951; paperback edition, New York: Delta, 1965.

It is not my central purpose as a compiler and editor to stimulate intellect or inspire debate. Rather, I would excite, enchant, and haunt you with the writings of these men and women. Particularly haunt—in the softest meaning of that word. So I hope that when you read, you will understand why I preface a book on psychotherapy with Paul Goodman's words: "Creator Spirit, come."

P.D.P.
New York
April, 1968

Contents

Contents

Recognitions in
Gestalt Therapy

Introduction
Dr. Erving Polster

A Contemporary Psychotherapy

This paper will describe some of the considerations which underlie contemporaneity and which have led me to Gestalt Therapy (1, 5) as an orienting system for my work.

Usually, words like "contemporary" or "modern" are applied only to the arts, such as architecture, painting, music, rather than to science. Yet science, and certainly psychotherapy, must also think in terms of the contemporary. Even truths that weave in and out of the generations make new marks every time.

Where new discoveries are made or old ones reformulated, there is a cultural lag during which the discovery is understood only by a few and seems relevant only to

3

a small portion of the population. Thus, the application of the new principles is delayed. During the time of lag the innovators of the new position, painfully confronted with the resistant or disbelieving society, need to devote considerable energy to managing this resistance so that the principles may become realized. During this period the protagonists become enamored of their own positions, and what begins as a justifiable manipulation on its own merit is inflated and labeled ultimate or universal. This exaggerated impact provides the adherents of the new view with the time, support, and continuity they need to gather acceptance for the application of their ideas. Then, however, more new discoveries are made which in turn face difficulties in becoming understood and in having their appropriate effect. At this point battles begin between the old-new and the new-new because the old has not had its chance to go all the way with its program.

Freudian psychoanalysis has been in this position for a good many years. Now that society has begun to understand its principles, many professionals have moved on, learning from the early masters, but changing according to the contemporary challenge and new discoveries. These facts of change and lag have especially confused those who see their work to be only a science, and thus presumably to have universal beliefs which must be defended *against* others. These workers forget that we view nature from only one perspective at a time. Only as long as we retain that perspective do we see nature as we do. If we shift, we see the world differently. Such shifting is necessary and lively and lies at the heart of contemporaneity.

Today the psychotherapist must integrate old insights into these new perspectives. He must distill a system unique for himself, consistent with prior formulations, yet not merely a static reënactment of what has gone before.

I. *Theoretical Changes*

Since we creatively advance processes begun in the past, the first requirement for contemporaneity is that we allow past accomplishments to illuminate our path. Only sometimes do we proceed from scientific discovery. More often we make artful choices based on having been touched by a huge range of effectors. Some of our greatest contributors have offered us only intuitive judgments. There were no proofs from Freud, nor from Jung or Adler, yet many of our great methodological and philosophical riches obviously come from them.

Looking further, since Freud there have been some great procedural inventors. Ferenczi required patients to *do* that which they feared, thereby bringing action into rhythm with the previous exclusively introspective methods in psychoanalysis. His work was a forerunner of the techniques of experimenting with life now so prominent, for example, in psychodrama and operant conditioning. Wilhelm Reich, going deeper than Ferenczi and meeting greater resistance, developed character analysis. His techniques concerning the body and his interpretation of details of the patient's behavior were important precursors to the contemporary interest among existential therapists in phenomenology and the deep self-experience.

Franz Alexander and Otto Rank were also important proceduralists, each in his own way making deep alterations in the core concept of transference. Alexander emphasized the importance of non-therapy experiences and broadened the interpretation of the transference phenomenon to include relationships outside the analytic office. This broadening was a tacit recognition of the therapeutic efficacy of day-to-day human relationships. Rank brought the human relationship directly into his office. He influenced analysts to take seriously the actual present interaction between therapist and patient, rather than to maintain the fixed, distant, "as though" relationship that had given previous analysts an emotional buffer for examining the intensities of therapeutic sensation and wish. Rank's contributions opened the way for *encounter* to become accepted as a deep therapeutic agent.

Also important historically is the advent of the here-and-now experience in psychotherapy. The here-and-now became important in four distinct movements before it was given crucial emphasis by the existentialists. These movements were: (1) *psychodrama*, which fostered growth through action, placing the individual into experimental scenes in which he could face with relative safety those aspects of the world that would not ordinarily be so safely available; (2) *the general semantics movement*, which treated language as a culminating life event, taken seriously for its own characterological nature; (3) *Rogerian psychotherapy*, whose techniques of reflection and clarification served to accentuate the presently existing conditions in the patient; (4) *group dynamics activities*, emerging from Lewin's theories about how people perceive and communicate with each other in groups. Thus, existentialism and existential psychotherapy had the road already paved when they came to prominence in the United States in the early 1950s. The new view of the primacy of present events in therapy was and is being assimilated by a constantly more receptive profession and public. In addition, these pre-existentialists expanded the relevance of therapy beyond those who were sick to people interested in their own growth and fulfillment, and they broadened professional practice beyond the limits of the psychoanalytic or psychiatric fraternities. In the light of obvious social need these may prove to be two of the most energizing innovations.

The existential philosophers supported a change in tone. They owed less to the Freudian system and could offer a new configuration for the splinters shooting off the Freudian mass. New bases for holism appeared.

First, cause and effect were no longer broken into two separate pieces. They came to have an interactive unity, not the disunity brought on by blaming the present effect on the past cause.

Second, symbols were no longer mere fronts for specific referents, but were appreciated for their impact as creative representations. It was recognized that symbols do not hide a separated referent but bring it into unity now, an indissoluble ingredient of the manifest moment.

A third holistic factor was the union of therapist and patient as participants in a two-way encounter, not in the separations previously enunciated by special dispensations to the therapist. By now the verity of each actual experience can be taken seriously for its own sake, not just as an intermediate circumstance standing between now and cure. The implicit faith is that good present experience has intrinsic healing power and need not be explained away.

II. *Social Needs*

The second requirement for contemporaneity in a psychotherapy is that it face the social needs of the day. There are many social needs; for example, those reflected in such present issues as interracial tension, delinquency, international mistrust, the poor quality of sexuality, psychologically sterile education, and the concern for authenticity in religious experience. The implications of psychotherapy theory for the solution of these social problems are profound and must be explored much further than they have been.

Let me consider one of these issues: the social need for new religious experience. By religious I mean not what is conventionally intended by that word, but rather man's concern with his self-experience, and his quest for coherence, unity, support, direction, creativity, microcosm. Man has always sought for these. In our time this search is impelled by the psychotherapeutic process, discovered through work with patients, but too relevant beyond pathological need to remain isolated from public concern.

Psychotherapy has often been described as a counterforce emerging from repressive religious principles. Freud denied the reality of God and described the obsessional nature of religious practices. He propelled man into a new view of his own true nature and rejuvenated his potency for facing it head-on. But the Judeo-Christian society, thus threatened, tried to isolate the new force he represented. Nevertheless, Freud raided the grand social unit and enfolded many of its members, one by one, in the most painstaking, prolonged, and devoted explorations of individual people in history.

But his early methods were not suitable as a community-wide process. First, the rituals, such as free association and lying on a couch were too private. Second, the generation was preoccupied with explanations, and although Freud and psychoanalysts generally knew the dangers of over-intellectualizing, their attitudes, times, and techniques were over-susceptible to it. Third, the theory and methods were socially non-activist and unconcerned with fostering good encounter among members of a group.

The need for arranged opportunities for this encounter is widespread. Witness the current expansion of group psychotherapy and related group processes as indicated in the reports of Hunt, Mowrer, and Corsini. Hunt (2) traces therapeutic progress from the early one-to-one transference of psychoanalysis to concern for "enrichment" in interpersonal relations, and ultimately to an authentic place for group psychotherapy in the concerns of social psychology. Corsini (1) documents the increasing impact of group psychotherapy by reporting that the number of publications on the subject has increased from 15 in the decade of the 1920s to 1,879 in the decade of the 1950s. Mowrer (3) in his recent book *The New Group Psychotherapy* reports a proliferation of so-called self-help groups, another sign of the undercurrent needs of the day. Although his views suffer from an overemphasis on confession, he is, nevertheless, an eloquent spokesman for psychotherapy in communion with others rather than only as a private, professional engagement.

The need for microcosm, a world set apart, which is basic to religion, exists also in psychotherapy. What cannot be done in the large society may be done in small communities. One seeks opportunities for new encounters unburdened by the anachronistic demands of a production system geared to achievements and leaving little room for simple being and growth. One needs to step off the conveyor belt to where indiscriminate obedience, secrecy, stereotyped language, and currying favor may be given up without inviting loss of job or friendship. As one patient said of her group meetings, "It is a time out of the week." Indeed, the therapy group provides an opportunity to say, "Stop the world. I want to get *on.*"

Thus, a group therapy with a unifying and liberating view can be a strong force for the development of good community, creating opportunities for self-renewal as well as chances to try out a new morality, permitting new ways of being together that are currently unsafe in the large society. Community, self-renewal, and morality are and always have been fundamental human concerns.

In our culture these factors have been most fully appreciated by the Judeo-Christian system, but they are now growing in relevance for the psychotherapeutic process.

Psychotherapy also offers the possibility of satisfying the important human need to symbolize. Symbolizing, inherent in religious experience, is fundamental in the psychotherapeutic process. Symbolizing serves man's need to condense and synthesize his inner processes by means of expressing, in one stroke, related, diverse details of his existence.

Community, self-renewal, morality, microcosm, and symbolizing are such lasting and compelling human needs that a respect for them permits even fruitless religious anachronisms to exist beyond their rightful day. Psychotherapy's rightful day is now. It must satisfy these lasting needs in today's way.

III. *Language*

What language is most useful and best understood? The early psychoanalysts had a language of their own that was impactful in its day. They had to create new words because their concepts were new. Some of them are: oedipus complex, libido, ego, id, superego, etc. Sometimes it was hard to tell whether the concepts were symbolic or concrete. There were arguments, for example, as to whether the id, ego, and superego were actual parts of the body or whether they were only abstracted convenient pictorial representations. Such arguments were no accident, since Freud used words that bridged the gap between science and religion and had both literal and symbolic qualities. Confusion was thus inevitable.

There are no longer the same demands for a language of psychotherapy. First, it is now possible to be less figurative and more concrete in descriptions of personality. Second, psychotherapists are beyond communicating to the technically and theoretically sophisticated. They are moving into the society and want to be understood by a greatly widened range of interested people. While Freud's words were classificatory, albeit dynamic, the current words tend to be more descriptive of *process*. The existential mode of therapy looks less for essences and tries to deal more with each individual actuality as it occurs. In Gestalt Therapy, which emerges from the existential scene, some of the key words are: awareness, contact, experience, excitement, encounter, emergency, unity, clarity, present, etc. These words are closer to everyday language and deal with those aspects of living which are the foreground concerns for people. This kind of language invites experience rather than explanation to be the core of living.

Pinning our nature down to categorical words such as neurosis, diagnosis, profession, repression, cause, patient, etc., results in deification of transitory lingual conveniences. All of these have an indispensable place in history, but they are only scaffolds. When we say someone has a neurosis or someone is a psychologist, we do say something important, but such technical terms usually communicate too readily, leading frequently to smugness and semi-understanding.

Common words are bothersome because they are not inherently or reliably "understood." Nevertheless, psychotherapy is composed of commonalities, and technical language all too often obscures real meaning. A man wants to tell about how softly his mother stroked his hair when he was crying, not about his oedipus complex. He searches for joy, perspective, effervescence, faith, vigor, scintillation, flexibility, delight, etc., not greater ego strength. Descriptions of process, appreciation of function, and awareness of self offer a framework for new sensitivity to that which is uniquely immediate.

IV. *Style and Repertoire*

The fourth requirement is freedom for the psychotherapist to function in a manner suitable to himself, using formulations that will permit him to develop a personal style and a ranging repertoire of procedures.

By style is meant the therapist's organization of personal characteristics, behavior, and taste which identify him as a unique practitioner. For one to have a desirable style is to be predictable in general character and also consistently surprising and fresh, both to one's patients and oneself.

Some people are more kind than others, some more verbal, some more permissive. Some make broad strokes, describing grand life processes and stimulating patients to awareness of large sections of their natures such as fear of death, gross lechery, noble generosity. Others may face tiny details of existence such as the way a patient uses the word "wish" rather than "want" in asking for a promotion or the way a particular position of his musculature affects his expressiveness. Clearly, variations in style must exist, theory notwithstanding.

A person must find a theory which is sympathetic to his best talents, whether they be interpretive, poetic, directive or such. If he doesn't do so, he will be inept, or more likely, phony. Each style has its advantages and disadvantages, and one must learn what particular problems are the consequences of his own style. One may know, for example, under what circumstances one is likely to make speeches to patients or laugh with them or refuse to answer questions. If one makes speeches, one may have to deal with resulting awe or fear or dependence. If one laughs readily, one must face possibilities of the patient's taking the process too lightly or making inconvenient buddy-buddy demands. If one refuses to answer questions, one may face resentments or feelings of abandonment. The primary question about the "rightness" of a style is whether one accepts responsibility for the consequences one evokes and is skillful in facing them.

Style and repertoire are closely related. Repertoire is the range of procedures from which the therapist may draw, depending for his choice on his sense of the immediate need and his intuitive guess as to the procedure most likely to be effective. Thus, the psychotherapist may at one time use such techniques as interpretation of dreams, productions of fantasies, free associations, various introspective exercises. On other occasions alternative possibilities are available: use of body language, role-playing, visual contact, voice integration, reports of experience, directed behavior, and patient-therapist contact.

Certainly, psychotherapists should be aware of the unlikelihood of discovering *the* single technique of psychotherapy. There are no such purified factors as "rationalism" in therapy or "operant conditioning" or "interpretation of dreams." These methods and others have been successful, but to put them on a competitive basis in terms of which is the *right* one is absurd.

Psychotherapists are people trying to find a way to work and some do better with some styles or procedures than with others. Systems of therapy that forget this become travesties. For instance, there is the story of the two psychoanalysts who were discussing a failure and saying that it happened because the patient was not required to lie on the couch in the first session. Such totemic sterility is widespread, and it is especially pronounced when the repertoire is so rigidly circumscribed as to prevent individual expression. Carl Rogers' early work was filled with such restrictive procedures, although his later existential orientation has expanded the range. His own depth of inner experience and sensitivity to his patients flowed within his early system of procedures, and this also has been true for many of his followers, certainly the effective ones. For many, though, such restrictions would have interfered with the fruitfulness of function.

However, the alternative to such limitations is not a

dilletante eclecticism. The former is absurdly competitive and doomed to stereotype; the latter is an empty shell, sterile even in knowledge. Variations in style and repertoire must cohere in a larger whole within which the psychotherapeutic exploration makes sense.

V. *Integrative Principles*

The fifth requirement of a contemporary psychotherapy is for integrative principles that bind previous historical directions together and orient the psychotherapist in what he is doing now.

Gestalt Therapy has such unifying characteristics, integrating existential and psychoanalytic insights with procedural inventiveness. It deals with three primary therapeutic devices: encounter, awareness, and experiment. Although these require extensive description, here is a brief sketch of each.

First is encounter, the interaction between patient and therapist, each of whom is in the present moment a culmination of a life's experiences. They may engage simply, saying and doing those things that are pertinent to their needs, the therapist offering a new range of possibility to the patient through his willingness to know the truth and to be an authentic person. Ideally this would be enough. It is curative for both to speak freshly, arouse warmth, and encounter wisdom. Contact of this nature may develop without self-consciousness or interpretation. But, of course, the resistances are great. Therefore, the encounter factors, potent as they are, usually require augmentation from the other two sources of therapy.

Second is awareness of bodily sensations and of the higher orders of self-experience such as emotions and values. Awareness is necessary for recovering the liveliness, inventiveness, congruence, and courage to do that which needs doing. Until one can accept strong inner sensations and feelings, one's expressions, verbal or physical, of anger, affection, disappointment, grief or the like will have little effect. Reduced living is the inevitable result of blocking internal self-experience. In Gestalt Therapy self-awareness is fostered through techniques requiring phenomenological articulations of self-experience. An inward look is required, one which goes beyond taking life for granted. This look encompasses the breathing process, tightness of sphincters, awareness of movement, and an infinite number of similar details ranging from small and physical aspects to larger awarenesses like expectancy, dread, excitement, relief, etc. All of these are directed toward re-discovering one's actual existence based on concrete experience rather than on logical deductions, like, "of course I'm breathing or I wouldn't be alive." In *Gestalt Therapy* by Perls, Hefferline, and Goodman there is an example of a young man exploring his own process of chewing food. He discovered a previously unknown feeling of disgust for food and noticed the way he desensitized his taste experience in order to avoid this feeling. The phenomenological discoveries one makes during such explorations grow into meaningful wholes. For example, a person may discover that his voice sounds weak when talking about his job or that he feels warmer inside than anybody realizes or that his neck tightens up frighteningly when he is surprised. He may discover a feeling of bewilderment during silence or embarrassment about saying goodbye.

The third therapeutic force is the experiment, a device which creates new opportunities for acting in a safely structured situation. Included are suggestions for trying one's self out in a manner not readily feasible in everyday life. For example, a progressive minister—calm, intelligent, and permissive—knows he does not reach his parishioners. Upon relating his hatred for the hellfire and brimstone style, and his own terror of it while growing up, his over-reaction to such a minister became apparent. He was asked to imitate such a sermon but to say what he himself might want to say to *his* people. After some resistance, the result was an electrifying sermon with deep impact, yet sensible and consistent with his own character. The experiment provides this opportunity for trying out varieties of behavior for which one may not be ready in everyday life. A safe emergency is created where, with the immediate help of the therapist, it may be more readily resolved. These experiments, if sensitively arranged, are graded in difficulty so as to be within the range of possibility but challenging enough to arouse resistances that may be faced and, hopefully, dissolved.

Out of these three interlocking areas a large diversity of specific techniques emerges, bound into a broad but delineated frame of reference. There is support for authenticity of personal experience for both therapist and patient. There is encouragement for inventiveness in technique. There is integration of action as well as introspection into the therapy process. And, finally, there is a return to the primary experience of self, the generic foundation of our existence.

REFERENCES

1. CORSINI, R. J., *Methods of Group Psychotherapy* (New York: McGraw-Hill, 1957).
2. HUNT, J. MCV., "Concerning the Impact of Group Psychotherapy on Psychology," *International Journal of Group Psychotherapy*, 1964, 14: 3–31.
3. MOWRER, O. HOBART, *The New Group Psychotherapy* (Princeton, N. J.: D. Van Nostrand, 1964).
4. PERLS, F. S., *Ego, Hunger and Aggression* (London: George Allen and Unwin, 1947).
5. PERLS, F. S., HEFFERLINE, R. F., & GOODMAN, PAUL, *Gestalt Therapy* (New York: Julian Press, 1951).

Paul Goodman

A Syllabus of Psychotherapy
(From *The Empire City*)

1.

"Please be aware of your breathing," said Antonicelli.

Horatio was troubled and saddened by what he had been hearing, and his breathing was coming a little unevenly and shallowly. Otherwise he was breathing nicely from his diaphragm like a great sad dog; he was sad but not at all anxious; his sickness was all in his head and in the world. "I'm breathing a little shallowly, and it's uneven," said Horatio. "There's a roughness in the bronchi and my heart is swollen. I'm sad." He sighed.

"Never mind the details. You're breathing, aren't you? That's what I want you to notice."

"Yes, I'm breathing. What about my breathing?"

"Ha, questions! Please notice your voice. Can you hear your voice?"

"What about my voice? It's sharp." His voice indeed had an edge of asperity.

"You're speaking, aren't you?"

"Yes, I'm speaking, but—"

"No buts. No buts and no ifs. That's just it—have you been listening to the sound of your voice?"

"Yes."

"There you go again. You've been listening. Breathing questions—speaking—listening. Probably listening at doors. Now notice: you're sitting there. You're looking at me—don't try to deny it; you're using your eyes. Stand up!"

Horatio stood.

Antonicelli struck his forehead as if in despair. "There you go again! Standing! Look at you! On your feet. Your legs are holding you up." He looked under the table. "Just as I feared—your feet are firmly planted on the ground."

Horatio sat down and closed his eyes.

"Now what are you doing?"

"Just collecting my wits."

"Collecting your *wits!* What *next?*" roared the doctor. "Next you'll be telling me that you have *thought* of something! And next you'll be *feeling* something—no, you've already done that. You yourself admitted that you were sad. Don't deny it. And where will you end up? I'll tell you. You'll end up by gathering some meaning or other, and that before very long."

"Yes, I have been thinking—" confessed Horatio.

"I knew it. My poor boy! You don't mind if I call you a boy, do you? It's a manner of speaking. Well, let's sum up; we might as well take it at its worst. There you sit *breathing all the time*, speaking on the outbreath, using your ears and eyes, sitting on your buttocks and even thinking of something now and then. Is it in a condition like that that you are going to make an adjustment to the social reality and expect to be a serious reader of the *Herald Tribune?* . . . Well, young man, what do you intend to do about it?"

"Is it—bad?"

"Bad? He asks if it's bad? From these things come the worst diseases!"

"Oh . . . I see what you mean—"

"Horatio?" said Antonicelli warningly. "Seeing? Meaning?"

Horatio fell silent.

2.

Antonicelli wrung his hands and sparkled away like a faulty connection. "The young man asks me if his functioning is bad. It can be fatal. There isn't a *single* maladjustment— I speak as a man of some experience— I have yet to come on a single social maladjustment that is not directly due to just such functions as you sit there exercising minute by minute in my office, and day by day outside of it. Don't deny it. Breathing, speaking, no doubt eating and excretion, imagination, locomotion, desire, feeling, sex—you do engage in sex, don't deny it.

What *not?* But especially the breathing, that's always the beginning. Always I find it has something to do with the breathing. It's a specialty of mine. If we could put a stop to the breathing, it might be possible to patch up the rest.

"Let me dwell on this. What's the usual situation? Something goes wrong. The patient comes to a physician. The physician refuses, he simply refuses, to see the whole situation. He tries to iron out this little kink, to straighten that quirk. A man has an ulcer and your physician pokes around with his diet; he has attacks of anxiety and palpitations and your physician tries to get him to take a decent breath of air. Et cetera, et cetera, et cetera. Empirics! Except that I happen to know something about the law—I have a little experience in that line too, ha, ha—I'd call it criminal malpractice."

"What do *you* do, Antonicelli?"

"There you go again, asking a question. This indicates curiosity, and even the folk wisdom knows the story on *that*. Curiosity killed a cat."

"What am I supposed to do?"

"You're supposed to sit there in a stupor while I blab; *anybody* knows *that*. . . . Look, Horatio, I am alarmed for you. It's going to be very hard for you to make an adjustment—I'll be frank with you. You realize you are a person of some concern to me; I am grateful to you. You saved me from the asphyxiation the time you stood there in court streaming round blue and orange with orgasms. I'll never forget it. So now I take you into my deepest confidence. You ask, what do *I* do? If thy right eye offends thee, pluck it out. That is the wisdom of the east. In these matters there is no help unless you get down to the root. You used to know that, try to recall it now. When a man can't stomach it any more, nothing will help but to stop eating. If he is sick at heart, stop the heart. And to speak generally, since with every function you exercise, you also inhale and exhale the environment around you, I would strongly urge you to practice inhibiting breathing.

"Let me pass on to you," he continued in a quieter voice, "the insight I got from old Professor Carlsen in Chicago. We students used to pester him asking about the deteriorating effects of tobacco, alcohol, and that shit. 'Boys,' he would say, 'don't worry about it. What makes a man die? It's joost living. It's joost living that wears the organism out.' "

"But—" said Horatio.

3.

"Counterwill!" thundered Antonicelli. "What do you think you're doing with your but?"

"I—" began Horatio.

"That proves it! Just as I thought. Now he says 'I.' I'll tell you exactly what you're doing. You're setting up your will against mine. So. You want to engage in a conflict, do you? A competition? Very well. (Remember you're paying for it.) Hop! Hop! Butt is what a goat does when it runs into something. You butt into somebody else's business. We also say a ham butt, a pig's ass. Well, don't think I'm going to let you thrust your ass into my face. Just notice what you're doing with your but. I confront you with my considered opinion, my advice to inhibit your living; and *you* promptly set up your counterwill—you don't like it. Now I'm not saying this is good and I'm not saying it's bad; here we don't indulge in moral judgments. But let's call a spade a spade. I can sniff a counterwill from Perry Street to the Menninger Clinic."

"But I—" began Horace.

Antonicelli threw up his hands.

4.

"I see I have been asking something too hard for you," Antonicelli began again, "something impossible for you to do. If I persist, I'll make even the possible impossible —it's a failing of mine. So let's withdraw a little and go step by step. Let's work simply on the little physical tricks till you get the idea. You'll get it, don't worry, have confidence. Just follow me, imitate me. Perhaps you're perplexed? Good, imitate me: let's express perplexity. Watch me. Raised eyebrows, forehead horizontally furrowed—and breathe! Don't stop breathing—when you're intensely perplexed, you might contract your scalp until your hairs stood up as if in fright."

Horatio was obediently making a face of intense perplexity.

"No! No!" cried Antonicelli. "I said look at me, follow me."

His own face was a dead-pan mask. "See? Do it like

this: you're intensely perplexed—" His face was a dead-pan mask and he was holding his breath.

Horatio began to be confused.

"Okay, perplexity is also too hard for you. So let's try worry. Deep vertical frown, quick irregular breath—think that you're going to *fail* in the exercise; you're going to lose the erection after all the trouble in getting her into bed. No! No! Watch *me!* Follow *me!*"

His face was a dead-pan; he was breathing quite at his ease.

"My God, man," he cried, "can't you even worry? Don't you feel *anything?* Are you completely dead?"

Horatio became annoyed. No one likes to be told that he's dead, even if it's a method of therapy.

"Okay, have it your way," said the doctor. "We'll try anger instead. Grind your teeth, jut your jaw on the outbreath—narrow flashing eyes—tightening fingers—but this time, please, really watch me and follow me."

Antonicelli's face was calm as calm and he began non-chalantly to clip his fingernails.

The clippings bounded off in odd directions, as they do.

As each one flew off, Antonicelli turned to watch it go, and he gave a little beck of his head when it landed.

He clipped another. It bounded away.

Naturally Horatio followed them too.

When there were no more, Antonicelli continued to follow them from side to side with a little beck of his head as each non-one didn't land. With a blank face, Horatio also followed them, and each time gave a little startled beck of his head.

"Good! At last!" said Antonicelli with deep satisfaction. "Now we're getting closer to the social reality. That's rage, in the world of the *Herald Tribune*. Shall we try love?"

But there was no need. For as soon as he found himself able to be aware of, to control, his behavior in the social reality, Horatio got the idea, and at once a warm tide of life flowed in his breast and he felt a terrible keen pang of air in his nostrils between his eyes. It would not require much for him to burst out bawling for his gone brother Lothar. He felt awful.

5.

Scenting the physicianly victory, Antonicelli flared his nostrils and was about to ask for a dream.

But it would have been a mistake at this point to press the patient further and seek to release the fullness of his misery. One has to learn to live with one's misery. And he himself didn't know, not he, Antonicelli, how to cope with the fact that we do not live in a golden age.

To let Horatio weep now might only awaken in him an intolerable unease, and he might have retreated as far as the world of the *Congressional Record*.

But it was hard for Antonicelli to err, since he had prayed to Aesculapius. Slowly the door of the closet was nudged open, and appeared the garnet eyes and the forked tongue of the serpent, warning him to end the session. The serpent slithered across the floor to the desk and reared his head up on the desk and looked at Horatio and Antonicelli, from one to the other, darting his tongue.

"Hello, hello," said Antonicelli. "This is Epidaurus my familiar," he said to Horace. "You see, I am an Asclepiad . . . I am only an Asclepiad . . . Yet Aesculapius, too," he said in a firmer voice and with dignity, "sailed on the *Argo,* with those friends. He was not just a professional."

Horatio took from his pocket the lump of sugar that he carried in case he should meet up with a horse. He offered it to the serpent, who ate it out of complaisance, though it was not his diet at all. Not at all.

"That's all for today, young feller," said Antonicelli. "Epidaurus tells me to break off. I think we're getting along famously. (By the way, what the devil does that expression mean?) Just practice by yourself (*a*) being at a loss, and (*b*) getting the feel and behavior of the social reality. When you have mastered these two, you'll have what you need for a perfect adjustment. . . . Just one more thing. Before you go home I'd like you to look in on Minetta Tyler, she's right across the hall in 4F. She and I are in collaboration, you know, but I'll let her explain how that works."

He stood up. "Good-bye, Horatio Alger," he said, and touched his shoulder and gave him a warm smile. "Cheer up. Hop! Hop!"

"Thank you, Antonicelli," said Horace.

Dr. Wilson Van Dusen

Existential Analytic Psychotherapy

Existential analysis is an example of a theoretical advancement which has far outstripped the development of actual techniques adapted to the new theory. There is no accepted technique of psychotherapy in existential analysis (1). The technique varies with the analyst. What remains is the same general program of how the patient should be regarded and understood. All such analysts will begin with an attempt to understand the phenomenological world of the other person. Beyond that there are wide differences in practice. In part these differences are fruitful since they represent a continued exploration unhampered by a dogma of technique.

Two points will be made here. The first is that there

is such an organic unity between the phenomenological approach and existential theory that the theory can and will be derived here from the basic phenomenological frame of reference. The second point is that there is a psychotherapeutic approach that most closely fits the theory. In fact, a close adherence to the theory demands a particular approach. The approach has been called Gestalt Therapy, and considerable credit for it is due to Dr. Frederick S. Perls (2, 3). So, in addition to rederiving existential analytic theory from its phenomenological foundations, we will show a psychotherapeutic approach that fits this theory.

The door to existential analysis is through phenomenology, and in this case the structure of the door implies much of the house. In the phenomenological approach to another person one attempts to understand his mode of being-in-the-world. There are a number of immediate and important implications. One does not come to his world with objective yardsticks or categories. One cannot translate his world into oral, anal, genital, id, ego, or superego terms unless the patient spontaneously sees these as real characteristics of his world. There is no objective, outside-of-him system into which one can fit his world. One must be ready to discover worlds radically different from one's own. The patient's world may be a holelike one out of which one crawls laboriously to look momentarily at daylight. His may be the seething restless world of the hipster (4) in which one swings from orgasm to orgasm in an attempt to break out of all boundaries. In every classificatory system our worlds differ relatively little, but in a phenomenological approach one encounters strange and radically different worlds. In therapy my own criterion as to whether I have understood the world of the other is whether or not he can recognize his world in my description.

The other day I examined a colleague's chronic schizophrenic patient in an effort to get more information for him about the patient. My colleague told the patient that I felt he was psychotic; the patient became angry and launched into a disturbed denial. Actually, I agree with the patient: he is not psychotic (the external-objective classification of him). Rather, he lives on the surface of his eyes and tongue because his brain and heart are paralyzed. Of course, the patient is technically psychotic, but in a phenomenological approach I don't wish to be technical. I told the patient that I really saw him as living in his eyes with a paralyzed brain, and he accepted this. Someone understood him. He felt my colleague so misunderstood him as to be psychotic himself.

This is the effect of the phenomenological approach. Insofar as one can describe the world of the other person as he finds it, the other person feels understood. Then one can work with him in full communication and interchange. From the paralyzed brain and heart we go to other aspects of his world. He feels safe. He is understood. Any sort of judgment or technical approach to his world leaves him with the justified feeling that the therapist is bending him to the therapist's own ends. One discovers the being-in-the-world of the other, with even the terms and all the subtle qualities of the world of the other. This does not imply I am in his world. At the end of the hour he goes back to his hospital ward or his home and I return to my other professional duties. He knows I do. He knows mine is a different world. But as he leaves the door he feels someone is beginning to understand how he feels. I don't need to pretend to be in his world. When he says that he is being poisoned, I can quite seriously accept that he feels poisoned and even explore the qualities and circumstances of this poisoning without pretending that I feel that poison is being slipped into his food. Usually he doesn't literally mean poison *qua* poison, and even if he does, our exploring of his poisoned world should open up other and more psychic aspects of poisoning.

So far we have said that the door into existential analysis is through an attempt to understand (not to judge or value) the being-in-the-world of the other. This understanding is in his terms, with his qualities. It is the opposite of any sort of objective or technical approach to him that, for instance, a diagnosis implies. He feels understood, not apprehended and bent by the other person. In this, one need not pretend to have a world exactly like his. One remains an individual with a different world. He doesn't feel he is with an expert with mysterious powers. He is with another person who is attempting laboriously and slowly to understand him. Nor is he with the lover who cries when he cries. The transference is less than in classical analysis. As one meets with and learns to describe the patient as he is here, one is also uncovering transference reactions. They too are described as part of his present being-in-the-world. They are discovered as they form and are described so that they won't have a hidden effect on the relationship. One could say that there is a continuous analysis of transference. This phenomenological entering into the being-in-the-world of the other is the foundation of existential analysis. It is so fundamental that the therapist who learns how to do this alone is very likely to discover spontaneously for himself all the other aspects of existential analysis.

There are a number of collateral discoveries once one has entered the phenomenological door. Most of science is an attempt to find static law. One finds that the world of the other is fluid and changing. The schizophrenic living in his eyes will be found to have a far richer and more complex world than appears at first sight. Also, it changes as we come to understand it. In one schizophrenic we explored a gesture as simple as his rubbing his nose. It was at first a filling up of a hole of nothingness (5). As we looked further it took on many and varied meanings. Not only is the therapist learning, but the patient is recalling in a gesture aspects of himself he had lost. We explore his style of movement, the changing emotional qualities in his voice, and his experiences here. Whereas he may have appeared simple to himself, he grows more complex, varied, and subtle in this exploration. A simple symptom takes on layers of emotional and interpersonal meaning. As we explore, his awareness expands. He is not the same person from moment to moment. Nothing has been done to him. He hasn't been interpreted. He has simply participated in a discovery of himself here.

Another implication is that one will not want to discard any part of his being-in-the-world. One will not look exclusively at the outer world as he sees it, or at the internal. Both are his world. He may live more in one or another sphere (the introvert-extrovert dichotomy). If the solidity and resistance of material things engages him then we will look at this. If a fantasy plagues him, then it is an important part of his world.

Dreams can be used as an important part of this discovery. Boss (6) makes the important point that dreams are not, strictly speaking, symbolic. They speak in a purely existential language. They tell what is currently critical in one's life by describing it in terms of dramatic events. Dr. Perls goes after the meaning of dreams by having the patient play-act all aspects of the dream until the patient is caught up in the events and thereby finds their meaning.

Also, one will not grasp the patient solely by his words (a tendency in many overly logical therapists). Features of his world are his bodily sensations, his use of his musculature, his gestures, his choice and use of clothes, and even the vocal inflections that underlie his words. Such a small matter as where he focuses his gaze is quite important. Does he communicate eye-to-eye with the therapist or is he talking to a potted plant in the corner? No part of his world is so small as to be meaningless. This approach to patients implies a much richer and more subtle understanding than the simple grabbing of another through his words. I would hope to be able to understand another person fully without having heard a single word of his. It would please me immensely to be able to imitate his movements and the sound of his voice, for then I have grasped some of his uniqueness.

In the exploration of the world of the other person one tends to center on the critical. In the past, experimental psychologists centered on unimportant aspects of the worlds of others. Look, for instance, at the vast number of studies of the two-point sensory threshold and similar works. They did this to grasp what could be translated into the modes of exact science. Because the psychotherapist is not attempting to catch what is measurable by science, he can afford to look at the critical. There is a most simple reason for the existential analyst's centering on the critical: the patient insists on it. The patient's life and destiny are at stake. He cannot help but present the critical, even though what he presents may look very peripheral to the therapist. The term "existential" has come to be nearly equivalent to the term "critical." How does one find the critical? By exploring all the aspects of the being-in-the-world of the other.

The space-time aspects of the world of the other person are found to be important. In classical Freudian psychoanalysis the analyst shifts the patient back into an exploration of the patient's history. In exploring the being-in-the-world of the other, one explores the world here, now. Only insofar as past or future are tangled in the world here-now do these become of consequence. After all, his world is here-now. It's not back in toilet training in childhood or forward in afterlife. He sits here before me and demonstrates his world. The centering in the here-now is a modern tendency coming into most therapies. Practically speaking, it causes an intensification and speeding up of therapy. There isn't the long escape into what Mama, Papa, or Sister did. "We are here. What are you doing now?" One need not wander for years examining aspects of the person projected in remote historical events. The person is here. We can study what he does here. In the hereness he shows how he chooses space, time, and the qualities of his world. One patient occasionally rubbed his hand across the bridge of his nose. It was perhaps two weeks before we began to understand this. The meaning was something like this: "I become anxious under your close regard (or anyone else's). In the anxiety, time and space suddenly develop a frightening hole. In the hole is nothing. I can't even remember. Nothingness. By touching my nose I am physically active and fill up the hole. Also I touch physical reality (my body) and come back to reality that way. Incidentally, my hand covers my eyes for a moment and your (analyst's) gaze is shut off for a moment." Here we began to discover his problem in a palpable way. It is with us here. It is not in the historical past. It is so palpable we can study it together now.

With the basic phenomenological approach, I believe, many others will discover that to some extent all study of past or future is a subtle abrogation of present responsibility. One cannot exclusively steer the patient into the present either. If the past or future intrudes into the session, it says something about how the patient is present. In the existential-analytic approach one doesn't steer the patient into past, present, or future. One discovers where the patient is now in his present being-in-the-world. It is a simple discovery in this approach that all psychopathology involves some degree of escape from the here and now into the spatially or temporally there, into otherness. The well-integrated person looks at the therapist, eye-to-eye, with security and composure, and chooses his being-in-the-world now. He is content to be here.

In this approach one will undo projections as fast as they form. The patient may ask, with some feeling, "Do you think therapy should go on indefinitely?" The patient is bothered and is projecting responsibility onto the analyst. The analyst can help bring the projection back to the patient by simply asking: "Would you make that into a statement?" The patient says, "You feel therapy should be interminable." There is a little more emotion in the voice and actions. Can the patient say it again clearer and more forcefully? "You feel therapy should go on forever!" After a moment the analyst can ask how the patient feels now. What was projected into the other is then discovered as arising from one's own emotions. Usually, the patient reacts after such an exchange as though he had been restored to power. The projection was not interpreted as a defect in the patient. The affect underlying it was recovered and the patient was restored to power.

There is no unconscious in this approach (7). Nothing is totally outside the realm of his present being-in-the-world when that world is examined in considerable detail and with considerable respect. One finds himself dealing with varying degrees of awareness from what is easily verbalized to not quite understood gestures to vague feelings that are not at first verbalized. Nothing is totally outside of his present being here (hence the term "dasein"—"being-here-analysis"). There are a great many ways of exploring the present. While the patient talks, something of an emotion may show in the eyes or voice, or he may make a gesture. When the emotion is strong enough to grip the person, then a simple noting of its presence by the analyst may help bring it to the fore. With a little help its expression becomes clearer. Something has been discovered in the testing ground of the present relationship. He finds and determines himself, rather than finds himself interpreted by another person. Well-handled, one can tell from moment to moment whether gains are being made because the pathology and the choices around it are here.

In this I am dealing with findings from the phenomenological approach which others may not have experienced yet. I am so secure in these findings, though, that I would be inclined to say that anyone who has learned to understand the being-in-the-world of others and is involved in their care in psychotherapy will of himself enter into existential analysis. At this point I would like to clarify what differentiates the phenomenological entrance from the inside of the house of existential analysis. In a few words, the entrance is phenomenological, the inside of the house is ontological, the essential nature of man (8). This was touched upon when we examined the critical and found it in the here and now. In the other (there, in time and space) it is hidden. One can center on the ontological, the critical, and the here and now by exploring the patient's choosing.

The patient's productions (words, actions, dreams, etc.) are all, so to speak, puppets. By examining his choosing here and now with me, I deal directly with the puppeteer. This is the existential engagement. He is caught. All avenues of escape are sealed. As he grows in awareness of the size and qualities of his world, his area of choice expands. In the beginning of therapy it appears he had no choice. He was caught as an actor in a repetitive, unpleasant drama. As awareness of his world expands he comes to deal with the playwriter—his forgotten choices. The drama changes. It appears more and more that he writes the drama. Therapy ends without any massive transference, because the therapist was no all-wise magician. He only permitted the patient to discover and choose himself.

In case it is not clear that this is relatively different from most other forms of psychotherapy, the difference will be underlined. Here there is no need to explore, or even to know, a patient's history. One could fully explore what is wrong here and what is chosen here without a history. In this approach there is no unconscious. His world is here. There are varying degrees of awareness in that world. There is no resistance or defense. This may be difficult to see, but both resistance and defense imply that one is outside the world of the other and makes an outsider's judgment of their world. There is no denial. To say that the patient is denying is to say that the analyst has a conception of the patient's world that does not match with the patient's world. The patient doesn't deny. He states what he knows of himself at the moment. In this form of therapy neither transference should ever become intense and burdensome, because this therapy is almost a constant analysis of transference, though even the term "analysis" is out of place here. One doesn't come to analyze (take apart) the world of the other. One comes to understand it. These few examples of differences from ordinary psychotherapy should suggest that this form of existential-analytic therapy is relatively new. It has historical roots in the work of Adler, Rank, Gestalt Therapy, and the work of Freud, but in itself it is a major shift in what is seen as psychotherapy.

Summary

Existential analysis is not yet identified with a particular therapeutic approach. By beginning with a phenomenological foundation, one can rederive the structure of existential analysis; by so doing, one discovers a technique that is particularly close to the theory of existential analysis. From phenomenology one learns to enter the present being-in-the-world of the patient without overlooking any of the qualities of that world. By centering in the present world one discovers the critical and the role of the patient's choosing. By this the patient feels understood and not interpreted, and discovers that he changes as the horizon of his present experiences expands. Starting from a phenomenological foundation, one rediscovers existential analysis and discovers that this analysis is a significant departure from classical therapies in several respects.

REFERENCES

1. May, R. *et al., Existence, A New Dimension in Psychiatry and Psychology* (New York: Basic Books, 1958, p. 77).
2. Perls, F. S., *Ego, Hunger, and Aggression* (London: George Allen & Unwin, 1957).
3. Perls, L., "Two Instances of Gestalt Therapy," *Case Reports in Clinical Psychology*, 1956, 3: 139–146.
4. Mailer, N., "The White Negro," in G. Feldman and M. Gartenberg (eds.), *The Beat Generation and the Angry Young Men* (New York: Citadel Press, 1958, pp. 342–363).
5. Van Dusen, W., "Wu Wei, No-Mind and the Fertile Void in Psychotherapy," *Psychologia*, 1958, 1: 253–256.
6. Boss, M., *The Analysis of Dreams* (London: Rider, 1957).
7. Van Dusen, W., "The Theory and Practice of Existential Analysis," *American Journal of Psychotherapy*, 1957, 11: 310–322.
8. Van Dusen, W., "The Ontology of Adlerian Psychodynamics," *Journal of Individual Psychology*, 1959, 15: 143–156.

Dr. Laura Perls

Two Instances of Gestalt Therapy

The two cases selected for presentation represent "typical" examples of a well-known clinical picture. Both patients come to therapy with similar complaints, namely, they have difficulties in contact and concentration. They are intelligent and gifted but second best. They cannot make adequate use of opportunities but think afterward of what they could or should have said or done. They find it nearly impossible to start anything new and waste a lot of time and energy on repetitive "dummy" activities. Both are self-conscious, feel awkward and ridiculous, think that most people don't care for them. Their concept of what they should be like amounts essentially to the ideal image of a near-Victorian lady or gentleman.

Their main support is their pride in the ability to do without. Nevertheless, there is in both an all-pervading feeling of frustration and dissatisfaction. In short, the diagnostic emphasis in both cases would be on the obsessional and more or less paranoid character features.

However, the similarity in diagnosis does not necessarily indicate a similarity in therapeutic procedure. I have chosen two cases for this discussion rather than a single one in order to demonstrate in greater detail the difference in therapeutic techniques which is necessary and possible by taking into account the uniqueness of the patient's contact (or avoidance) techniques and the availability (or lack) of support functions.

The assumption of contact and support functions does not, as it may appear at first glance, reintroduce a dichotomy into the holistic concept of the functioning of the organism but is a differentiation according to the figure-ground principle. Contact—the recognition of "otherness," the awareness of difference, the boundary experience of "I and the other"—is more or less alert, specific, concernful awareness and activity. It is so much "figure" in the organismic functioning that neurosis has been defined as *avoidance of contact*, and the different types of neurosis as different *stages of withdrawal* from or limitation of contact.

But "who is all eyes does not see." The contact functions—by way of a specific organ or a specifically structured activity—take place against a background of organismic functions that are normally unaware and taken for granted; yet these latter provide the indispensable support for the foreground function of contact.

43

They comprise hereditary and constitutional factors (primary physiology, etc.); acquired habits that have become automatic and thus equivalent to primary physiology (posture, language, manners, techniques, etc.); and fully assimilated experience of any sort. Only what is completely assimilated and integrated into the total functioning of the organism can become support.

Thus, contact and support are not identical with Conscious and Unconscious. The Unconscious, as far as it is repressed and introjected, is not support but the very lack of it. It is interference with and blockage of successful contact.

If we redefine neurosis as a state of malcoordination of contact and support functions, and the different neuroses as different types of malcoordination, we may define the goal of therapy as the achievement of optimal coordination of contact and support functions. We also may in time, with further research, arrive at the realization of a functional typology of neurosis.

At this point I find the contact/support concept a useful tool in the therapeutic situation. It immediately takes into account the patient's total behavior, not only his history and his verbalizations. The patient learns to work with material that is immediately available to him in the actual situation, without speculation or interpretation, by taking stock of all the aspects of his actual behavior, by bringing into the foreground and making figure out of what usually remains unrealized in the background. The questions "How?" or "What?" or "Where?" or "What does this do for you right now?" take preference over "Why?" or "What for?"; description prevails

over explanation, experience and experiment over interpretation. Working strictly from the surface, *e.g.*, from
the actual awareness at any given moment, we avoid the
mistake of contacting depth material prematurely that in
the first place was and had to be "repressed" because at
a certain point in the patient's history it was unsupport-
able. Making it available by interpretation of dreams or
symbolic actions does not mean making it more usable
but often causes a strengthening of the defense mecha-
nisms, waste of time or, worse, loss of the material by
projection. The "negative therapeutic reaction," like the
negative reaction to any other experience, is the result
of unsupported contact.

On the other hand, the strengthening and expansion
of the support functions mobilizes the alienated emotions
and potentialities for contact, and makes formerly repressed depth material easily accessible. The process
could be compared with the creation of a work of art
(the highest form of integrated and integrating human
experience) in which the conflict between a multitude
of incompatible and unmanageable experiences is realized only at the point where the means for its interpretation and transformation become available (1).

How the concepts of contact and support are applied
in therapy will become more evident in the actual case
discussions.

1. The Case of Claudia

Claudia, a twenty-five-year-old Negro, comes from a
lower-middle-class West Indian background. The family

is socially ambitious in a Victorian way; they try to emulate white society and to segregate themselves from "black trash" by strictness of morals and manners which in actual white society do not apply anymore. They are religious in an obsessional-conventional way.

Her father was domineering and rather brutal; he left the family when Claudia was about twelve to follow Father Divine. She has no contact with him now. Once terrified of him, she now feels only contempt. Her mother is meek and submissive, self-sacrificing, religiously moralizing. Her younger sister is pretty, feminine, soft, motherly-protective. A younger brother committed suicide while in jail for an alleged and likely homosexual involvement.

The patient regards herself as emancipated. She is very intelligent, has a degree in social science, is a caseworker with a city agency. She is coffee-colored, tall and slim, quite attractive but indifferently dressed and made up. She is well-behaved, uses "refined" language, is principled as to "what a young lady can or cannot do." Motorically, she is rather jerky; her voice has a hard edge to it. She is bony and rather flat-chested, her head thrown aggressively forward, the muscles in her broad, boyish neck tense. She lives at home with mother, sister, and aunts, whom she scares and bullies, and a righteous, religious uncle, whom she despises and is afraid of.

She comes for therapy because she is "just not good enough at anything." She is not interested enough in her work; she is afraid of and feels contempt for her clients. She gets behind in her casework. She cannot concentrate on her studies and had to repeat several exams. Socially, she is awkward and unhappy. People don't like her; they seem to be scared of her. She cannot get hold of the "right" people; she cannot be alone, either. She diagnoses herself as paranoid and is afraid of insanity. Occasional suicidal fantasties are reported which she herself does not take very seriously. More serious are headaches, which bother her at times for a period of several days. She complains that she cannot wear feminine clothes and that she dreads going to dances and parties looking silly in frilly dresses. Nevertheless she goes, suffering agonies. The patient has no manifest sex life, feels vaguely excited by and vaguely attracted to both sexes. She condemns both inclinations, feeling wanton and sinful with the one, weird and perverted with the other.

She is also subject to numbers of obsessional rituals and habits, among them a severe hand-washing compulsion, which she does not even mention. As these habits are her safety devices, her support attitudes, they are automatic and taken for granted. In spite of the emphasis on how sick, weak, and confused she feels, and how she suffers, the patient gives the impression of competence, articulateness, and great strength.

The patient was seen once a week for three separate periods of seven to eight months since 1949. The interruptions were due partially to time and money reasons but more because of her inability to restart after long vacations or even after a week's interval. From 1952 to 1953, after she had achieved a certain level of functioning, I did not see her until she returned, voluntarily, at the end of 1953 to work through some difficulties that she had become aware of in the meantime. Since then, she has been working steadily, more and more concentrated and successfully, and is rapidly approaching the end of her treatment.

But we shall go back to the beginning. Her first sentence, after she had plunked herself down on the couch was, "I am in a bad way, doctor. You'll have to do something for me. I doubt if you can. You won't be any better than Dr. X. [a psychiatrist with whom she had worked for a short period and who had sent her to me]. She couldn't do anything with me," etc., etc.

It was obvious that the patient was challenging and taunting me. She was making demands, telling me how to handle her, trying to dominate and control the situation. Of course, from her family history it became quite evident that she identified with the bullying father and tried to manipulate me into the role of the submissive, hardworking, despised mother. But during the first few minutes of the first interview I did not have this information and I did not need it. I had only to consult my own reactions to the patient's behavior, my awareness of being belittled and imposed upon, the feeling of hostility that she provoked in me, to realize the specific pattern that the patient was acting out in this meeting as well as in any other contact situation. For her it was a contest in which she had to get the better, a question of victory or defeat, nearly of life and death. When she is unable to control the situation, she gets confused and anxious and has to withdraw.

If I had allowed her to ramble on in the same vein, she would have felt only that she was getting away with it again, that is, it would have increased and fortified her contempt for the feminine sex and with it her own basic inferiority feeling. If I had pointed out that she was telling me my business, but that I was the doctor and conducting the therapy, I would only have provoked a sharpened contest, as she would have been quite unable to cope with the ensuing confusion. In fact, whenever she felt that I was in some way getting the better of her, she ran back to her former analyst and usually succeeded in manipulating her either into accepting her for a visit or at least an hour-long telephone conversation to gain reassurance of her own superiority. Thus, in the first few weeks of working with me, she went back frequently and without telling me about it. At later stages she went sporadically and told me in the next session, at first brazenly, "I went to see Dr. X. . . . So what do you have to say to that!" and later on, more and more embarrassed, "[smile] you know, [wriggle] I called Dr. X. [blush]!"

In the first session, neither withdrawing from nor entering into the contest pattern that the patient tried to impose on the situation, I asked her if she really wanted help. "Yes, of course, that's what I am coming for." I pointed out that she was asking for help in a rather peculiar fashion, not really asking for something that under the circumstances she might reasonably expect but demanding it as if I were trying to withhold something from her and she had to assert her right to get it—"you better, or else!" She did not really know me, yet she tried to pigeonhole me, put a label on me from her store of past experience and to fantasy what I was or was not going to do in the future. The only thing that she did not do was to consider me here and now (face to face), to look at and listen to me, to make contact with me and find out about me in this present actual situation. For a moment the wind was taken out of her sails; she was deprived of her habitual support. She got a little confused and embarrassed but quickly collected herself, threw her head forward, and barked, "I don't know anything about your qualifications. Do you have any? For all I know you may be a quack!" I satisfied her curiosity in this respect, but then pointed out that again she had looked for reassurance from the past (this time *my* previous experience and training) rather than through an evaluation of whatever she could experience of me and through me in the present.

The following weeks and months were spent mainly in concentrating on the here-and-now experience. The patient was discouraged from dwelling too much on her history and family background. It soon became more and more evident to her that she used the past as a convenient excuse and justification, and that she burdened the family with the whole responsibility for whatever she was now, so that she need not make any effort toward any relevant change now, in the present. The questions "What effort?" or "Effort against what?" mobilized intensive work on her so-called laziness and lack of concentration and contact. It was pointed out that contact can be made easily and adequately only when support is adequate and continuous. The obvious *discontinuities* in her behavior, her jerky motions, the break in her voice, her shallow arhythmical breathing, her separation of head (mind) and body (animal), her double moral standards, her masculine superiority fantasy against the reality of her femininity, to name only a few, were all in turn brought into the foreground to that degree of awareness at which, if not an immediate change, at least an experimental approach, a fantasy, or homeopathic play with different modes of behavior became possible.

The inability to concentrate for any length of time provided the first opportunity to make her aware in more and more detail of her techniques of self-sabotage. She came to therapy apparently with great interest in helping herself, but very soon in every session got either bored and somewhat foggy, erratic and distracted by incidentals. She said, "I can make some sort of a start [her head pushed forward, her voice raised, her eyes piercing], but then . . ." (the head drooped, she looked squashed, the voice fizzled out, the sentence remained unfinished). A whole series of experiments was conducted around every detail of this "half-experience." She learned to pay attention to the sound of her voice and how she produced it. The voice did not carry through, as she gave herself no chance to re-inhale during the act of speaking. The rhythm of breathing became arrested, the diaphragm got fixed at the bottom of the exhalation, and the voice had to be pushed out from the throat with great tension in neck, face, and throat muscles. She found that her speech was not really an expression, it did not come from the center (that is, from balanced posture and a continuity of rhythmical breathing, the indispensable support for optimal functioning), but it was a "pre-tense" in the literal sense of the word (coming from head and neck only). Listening to her voice, she recognized spontaneously, with a shock, "I sound like my father—raucous, bullying." Then, without pushing from the top, "And I shut up like my mother—confused, stupid." Her breathing became deeper, more rhythmical, she felt her "stomach getting warm. Now it is fluttering and twitching." And she started to cry. Thus, from the increasing self-awareness in the actual therapeutic situation, without digging into memories and without interpretation, the patient realized the double identification with both parents and the resulting inner conflict together with the means of resolving it.

Her motoric awkwardness and jerkiness also were revealed as part and parcel of the masculine pretense. Just as in conversation and argument only the head and voice came forward, so in actual motion in any direction or toward any object only the extremities moved, or rather jerked, while the torso remained rigid and the center of gravity (the pelvic region) was retracted. The joints were tight; there was no spring action and no swing in her movements. Since she is tall and lanky, she looked and felt not just awkward but grotesque. With increasing awareness and with the help of detailed exercises she acquired gradually more and more mobility, more continuity in breathing, more fluidity in motion. She felt "more energy, more confidence, more swing, more stride, more excitement." She started to play tennis and soon became quite proficient. She worked more easily and with greater interest, and she made new social contacts.

At this stage she went through an intense homosexual

phase. She still maintained a predominantly negative concept of femininity, together with a comparative rigidity and insensitiveness of the pelvic region. During the last few months—after we had worked through her initial disgust barrier (which in turn led to some work on her eating and learning habits, her indiscriminate stuffing and gobbling and swallowing of food as well as of information and principles and her feeling "fed up")—she has developed more and more sensitiveness and flexibility in her middle region and with it a greater acceptance of herself and her possibilities as a woman. She has become interested in and excited by men and has lately had some intimate heterosexual experiences. She does not feel too confident yet, and it will take her some time to develop more positive feminine "techniques."

Her former brazenness, the pretense of strength that is not centrally supported, has given way to genuine embarrassment, the awareness of a temporary malcoordination of contact and support functions, which means uncertainty, curiosity mixed with reluctance, a little anxiety, and a lot of excitement. The patient's physical appearance has changed considerably, quite apart from the changes in posture and coordination. Her bone structure, of course, is the same, but her bust is more developed, her thighs are heavier, her face is more relaxed and looks rounder. Her menstrual period, which was usually early (twenty-three days), had become at first retarded (thirty-three to thirty-five days) and now more normal (twenty-eight to thirty days). She has found her own style in clothes which is feminine in a sporty way, without frills, quite smart. She has, at least for the time being, given up her job as a social worker and taken up library work. She feels that it gives her more support in the process of learning to handle herself with her own problems than did her previous effort to manipulate other people with their difficulties. She has left her family's home and moved into a boarding house near the place where she is working. She is now considering sharing an apartment with a friend. Claudia has become in fact what formerly she only imagined, but in some way always wanted to be, an emancipated female.

2. *The Case of Walter*

Walter, forty-seven years old, is a Central European Jewish refugee. He comes from an impoverished middle-class family, which nevertheless provided him with a university education. He became a lawyer, but with his degrees invalid in the successive countries of his emigration, he had to enter business life.

His father was an unsuccessful businessman, colorless, meek, and mild, with no initiative. His mother was ambitious and domineering, bitter about the father's failure. She was irritable, inconsistent in her demands, more amiable when the son finally achieved some professional and social status. She died in an asylum following a complete paranoiac breakdown in the emigration. A younger brother is happy-go-lucky, apparently unaffected by the family situation.

The patient is married to an intelligent, subtly manipulating woman. They have two children, one of whom is slightly spastic. Walter is fond of the children, but feels he does not handle them well; he is too anxious, too constraining. The originally quietly companionable marriage has lately become somewhat precarious. His wife, interested in psychology by way of the child's handicap and therapy, is undergoing therapy herself and becoming increasingly dissatisfied with their relationship, mainly with his indifference to her interests.

The patient looks tired, resigned, and old. He walks with a slight stoop, elbows tight to his body, feet shuffling. His expression is intelligent, but worried. The eyes dart furtively around looking for an "out," the mouth is set in an apologetic smile. His speech is hesitant, he talks only "when he is spoken to." The voice is monotonous, has a wailing quality.

He is dissatisfied and in a dull way unhappy with nearly everything in his life. He is not so much complaining as berating himself for being such a failure in business, in social contacts, in family life. He postpones everything that is not strictly routine, minor business phone calls as well as major decisions. He dreads meeting people, has to break his head for something to say, feels awkward and self-conscious. He is afraid of losing old business connections and convinced of his inability to make new ones. In spite of all these obvious limitations and self-recriminations, the patient is not unsuccessful in business, makes a comfortable living as an agent for some foreign business concerns, has kept the same accounts for many years, and is appreciated for his reliability and foresight. His children love him. He also has a small number of good friends. He gets great enjoyment from being out in the open, in contact with nature. But this more positive information was not available at the beginning of his therapy.

The patient was seen twice weekly for about four months (March through June, 1953), then once weekly, with an additional weekly group session, for ten months. Group therapy proved particularly effective in this case, and the patient is still a member of a therapy group, while his individual treatment has been terminated.

In his first interview the patient stumbled into the room not looking right or left, as if he were wearing blinkers. He sat down at the edge of a chair, literally "on edge," squirming, saying nothing for several minutes. To my question, "What brings you here?" he clasped his arms tightly, shrugged his shoulders, finally mumbled diffidently, with a faint undertone of irritation and nagging, "I don't know what I am coming for. . . . My wife thinks I should. . . . I don't think it is of any use. . . . I don't know what to say. . . . My wife says . . . ," etc., etc. (*shrug, collapse*).

I felt somewhat squashed, too, and a little bored. The patient had, at least for the moment, achieved his neurotic aim, he put me off, he bored me with his monotonous wail and his repetitiousness; in fact, he did his best to discourage me from becoming interested. Obviously he regarded the whole situation as a nuisance and wanted to be left alone. But in presenting this entirely negative front, he also exposed in detail the techniques that supported his withdrawal pattern and thus, quite unintentionally, provided me with exactly what he so desperately tried to withhold, the very "handle" by which he could be reached.

As in the case of Claudia, it was pointed out to the patient that his way of asking for assistance was not too well designed for actually obtaining it, and that if anything, it watered down whatever interest one might develop in doing anything for him. "Yes," his voice sounded much stronger now, nearly defiant, "I know I am boring. I never know what to say. I don't like asking people for anything. I always worry what they expect of me. I have to figure out what I should say; it takes too much time and I know only afterward what I should have said."

Considering the question of how all this applied in the actual therapy situation, the patient discovered that he was always so busy anticipating other people's needs and demands or berating himself for having missed out on something in the past that he had no chance to realize his own needs and interests and actions in any present situation, even when it was specially designed for no other purpose but his own self-realization.

It took a number of months to make him realize that what he felt was not, as he maintained, "nothing," but was rather discomfort, tension, impatience, irritability, distrust, apprehension; that what he did also was not "nothing," but was rather pulling himself together, suspending animation, waiting for something to be over, whether it be a business meeting, an argument with his wife, or a therapy session.

Listening to his voice, the patient found to his surprise not only that he sounded like his father (a fact that he had always known) but also, particularly when he was berating and belittling himself, that he sounded like his mother having an argument with his father. The suspended animation attitude was thus revealed as a most adequate support for the child to keep out of an unmanageable and unsolvable conflict. The ensuing desensitization led to the introjection of and identification with that very conflict, and in turn to an externalization, which transformed every contact situation into a potential threat.

Even when he succeeded in mobilizing his voice on his own behalf, it was mainly in the service of keeping out of reach, of escaping from some imposition or responsibility that might possibly be put on him. He was most emphatic in saying, "I can't!" "I am not able to . . . ," "I don't know!" The tone of his voice left no doubt that what he was really expressing was "I won't!" But he had found a technique by which he did not have to realize, and therefore did not have to feel guilty about, his own spitefulness.

It was comparatively easy to make the patient sensorially and intellectually aware of *what* he was doing, *what* he was doing it *for*, that his techniques provided support for *withdrawal* from undesirable and unmanageable experiences in the *past*, that they *now* constituted a blockage and *interference with the desired contact*. It was very laborious and took many months of concentration and a great number of experiments and exercises around every detail of his withdrawal techniques to get the patient to that degree of *motoric* awareness at which he became able to make a relevant change.

5 8

In Claudia we found a certain mobility of the extremities unsupported by the more central coordination of posture and breathing; in Walter we find hardly any mobility at all. He was all in one piece, literally pulled together. Claudia had the possibility of comparing the rigidity of her back, chest, and pelvis with the jerkiness of the extremities, and consequently she could experiment with the extension of both modes of moving in either direction, until she had achieved some continuity of coordination and flexibility. But Walter had nothing to compare—that is, there was not enough difference in his motoric experience to make any particular movement or tension foreground figure, nothing except the shrug of the shoulders. From the awareness of the shoulder shrug, the stock-taking expanded. The patient experienced the comparative mobility of the shoulders as against the rigidity of the adjoining regions—neck, arms, chest. He spontaneously recognized the shrugging not just as a symbolic gesture but as an actual motoric expression of "I can't!" or "I don't know!"—the onset of a movement without reach, without direction, without continuity. Experimenting with reach, continuity, and direction, the patient realized that he did not make any outgoing movements at all, that he was completely pulled together in the vertical, and had no expansion whatsoever in the horizontal direction, no flexibility of the neck, no swing or lift in his arms, no buoyancy, no stance, no stride.

When, after several months of awareness experiments and exercises, he had partially succeeded in loosening up, his dutiful schoolboy attitude ("My wife thinks . . . ,"

"My analyst says . . . ," "I know I should . . .") changed to real interest and curiosity. He became easier with people and much friendlier. At this stage he went through a period of intense embarrassment. He was encouraged to admit and express the embarrassment rather than to withdraw from the embarrassing situations or, worse, to stick them out with grim determination. It was pointed out that embarrassment is the inevitable awareness of lack of support that accompanies the initial exciting contact with any new experience. Thus, it is the emotional state applying to all stages of rapid growth and development. It is typical for the small child at a certain stage as well as for the adolescent. It is due to a lack or an unawareness of adequate techniques to cope with the new experience. If one can stay with the situation in spite of or, better, *with* the embarrassment, he has a chance, by discovering and developing new support attitudes, to make more successful contact with the new experience and thus to overcome the embarrassment. If, on the other hand, one avoids the embarrassment either by withdrawing from possibly embarrassing situations (like Walter) or by brazening them out with a pretended courage (like Claudia), he will never acquire new valid support techniques—that is, he will have to confine his contact experiences either in fact (like Walter) or in sensitivity and consequence (like Claudia).

For several weeks Walter felt and behaved like an adolescent; he blushed and giggled and his voice changed. In a few instances, when the discrepancy between his new involvement and the lack of support, mainly the rigidity in his diaphragm and his upper arms, became too overwhelming, he became quite hysterical, laughing and crying and wildly gesticulating. He was able to recognize the attack afterward as the spontaneous mobilization of these most inflexible and insensitive parts of his organism (the hysterical attack is probably a motoric emergency reaction of the total organism, just as yawning is in the case of oxygen deficiency). Consequently, he could extend this awareness into more and more co-ordinated mobility.

At this stage group therapy became the most effective agent in the patient's development. At first he balked at even remotely considering the possibility of taking part in a group. But gradually he agreed, at least intellectually, that it might be a desirable step. Finally, he joined, at first very shyly sitting on the fringe, a silent observer. He refused even to take the most minor part in any psychodramatic experiment. But soon, encouraged by his observation of other group members, he began to admit and express his own uneasiness and embarrassment.* It

* This is also in contrast to Claudia, who had to control and dominate the proceedings from the very beginning. When her brazenness and phoniness were attacked, she had no support at all and could not face her embarrassment. She attended only very few meetings and dropped out of her group (1952) after one of the members had pointed out the senselessness of her hand-washing compulsion by showing her the dirt on her hands through a magnifying glass. A few weeks ago she returned to the group of her own accord, more interested, more observant, more cooperative.

was in the group situation that Walter became fully aware of how vigorously and emphatically he insisted on being ignorant and incapable. He recognized it as a rather clever and, in its own way, competent avoidance technique. From here on it was only a few steps—via some experiments with direct mutual criticism among the group members and an exciting psychodramatic experience where he acted his mother shouting, scolding, and slapping a little boy—to a greater realization of his own present-day contact with people, his own interests, opinions, criticisms, needs, demands.

With increasing self-awareness he simultaneously became more genuinely aware of others, too. He no longer has to figure out what is expected of him, he responds immediately to the situation, and resists vigorously when he feels imposed upon. He is intelligently helpful to anyone in need; to everybody's great surprise, he was the only one who, when one of the group members stormed out of the room in a fit of anger and tears, went the next day to visit her to find out if she was all right.

Today he is the "father" of the group, benevolent, a little reserved but not shy, dignified without being stuffy, critical without nagging, quite gay with a keen sense of humor. His family relationships have improved; he enjoys the children (the child's therapist is delighted with his patience and understanding); he shares more interests and experiences with his wife. His business contacts are much easier; he feels more confident and less apprehensive; his income during the last year has substantially increased. At present he is abroad, an honored house guest of someone whom formerly he was afraid of as his boss, but now appreciates as his client. He acts his age and he looks ten years younger.

REFERENCES

1. Perls, Laura, "The Psychoanalyst and the Critic," *Complex 2*, 1950.

Paul Goodman

Human Nature and the Anthropology of Neurosis

1. *The Subject-Matter of Anthropology*

This is an essay in abnormal anthropology. The subject-matter of anthropology is the relationship between man's anatomy, physiology, and faculties and his activity and culture. In the seventeenth and eighteenth centuries, anthropology was always so studied (climaxing, probably, in Kant's *Anthropology*): for instance, What is laughter? how does it culturally manifest itself for man's well-being? More recently anthropologists lost sight of the relationship as their special study, and their books display a quite astonishing split into two unrelated sections: Physical Anthropology, the evolution and races of man; and Cultural Anthropology, a kind of historical sociology. For instance, it is an important proposition of Cultural Anthropology that technical innovations (*e.g.*, a new plow) diffuse rapidly to neighboring areas, but moral innovations diffuse slowly and with difficulty. But this proposition is left groundless, as if it were part of the nature of these cultural objects, rather than shown to be part of the nature or conditioning of the animals involved, the men carrying the culture, these men, in turn, being shaped by the culture they carry. Most recently, however, owing mainly to the impact of psychoanalysis, the classical animal/cultural interrelationship is again being studied, in terms of early child training, sexual practices, and so forth. And from the point of view of abnormal psychology, we here offer some biological/cultural speculations.

2. *The Importance of this Subject for Psychotherapy*

We can see the importance of the anthropological question "What is Man?" if we consider that medical psychology owes a difficult double allegiance. As a branch of medicine it aims at "merely" biological health. This includes not only healthy functioning and absence of pain, but feeling and pleasure; not only sensation, but sharp awareness; not only absence of paralysis, but grace and vigor. Dealing with a psychosomatic unity, if psychotherapy could achieve this kind of health, its existence would be justified. And in medicine the criteria of health are fairly definite and scientifically established;

we know when an organ is functioning well. This aspect of "human nature" is unambiguous.

But there is no such thing as "merely" biological functioning (for instance, there is no such drive as "mere" sex, without either love or the avoidance of love). So medical means are insufficient.

Once beyond medicine, however, the very aim of therapy, the norm of health and "nature," becomes a matter of opinion. The patient is a sick man, and man is not finally known for he is always changing himself and his conditions. His nature is surprisingly malleable. Yet at the same time it is not so completely malleable that the nature can be disregarded, as some democratic sociologists and fascist politicians seem to assume; it is also surprisingly resistant, so that suddenly there are neurotic reactions of individuals and a stupidity, torpor, and ridigity of the average.

In psychotherapy, moreover, these changes of condition are all-important, for they are what engage a patient's interest; they involve his fears and guilts and his hope of what he will make of himself. They rouse his excitement—they are the only things that rouse excitement—they organize awareness and behavior. Without these peculiarly "human" interests there is no biological health and no way of achieving it by psychotherapy.

3. *"Human Nature" and the Average*

So the doctor beats about for models and theories of what is humanly enlivening. This is why Freud insisted that not medical men but, with medical collaboration, literary men, teachers, lawyers, social workers make the best therapists, for they understand human nature, they mix with ideas and people and have not been content to waste their youth acquiring a specialty.

The task would, of course, be immensely easier if we enjoyed good social institutions, conventions that gave satisfaction and fostered growth, for then these could be taken as a rough norm of what it means to be a full man in the specific culture; the question then would be one not of principles but of casuistical application to each case. But if we had reasonable institutions, there would not be any neurotics either. As it is, our institutions are not even "merely" biologically healthy, and the forms of individual symptoms are reactions to rigid social errors. So, far from being able to take fitness to social institutions as a rough norm, a doctor has more hope of bringing about the self-developing integration of a patient if the patient learns to adjust his environment to himself than if he tries to learn to maladjust himself to society.

Instead of a dynamic unity of need and social convention, in which men discover themselves and one another and invent themselves and one another, we are forced to think of three warring *abstractions:* the mere animal, the harried individual self, and the social pressures. The normal person either keeps himself unaware of this raging war within his personality, does not notice its manifestations in his behavior, and keeps it fairly dormant, or he is aware of it and has concluded an uneasy truce, snatching at safe opportunities. In either case there is much energy spent in pacification and valuable human powers are sacrificed. In the neurotic person, the conflicts rage to the point of exhaustion, contradictions, and breakdown—nor can it be concluded that he was therefore in some way weaker than the normal, for precisely stronger gifts are often socially disastrous. There is an important difference between the normal and neurotic, but it is not such that when a neurotic comes as a patient and poses an earnest *practical* problem for the doctor, the doctor can set as his goal a normal adjustment, any more than he could give an arrested tuberculosis a clean bill of health, though he might have to discharge the patient. Rather he must hope that, as the patient begins to reintegrate himself, he will turn out to be more "human" than is expected, or than the doctor is.

(Further, we must remember that in the present run of patients of psychotherapy, the distinction between normal and neurotic has become less than irrelevant; it is positively misleading. For more and more of the patients are not "sick" at all; they make "adequate" adjustments; they have come because they want something more out of life and out of themselves and they believe that psychotherapy can help them. Perhaps this betrays an oversanguine disposition on their part, but it is also evidence that they are better than the average, rather than the reverse.*)

* We have mentioned above that the selected run of patients is an intrinsic factor in the various psychoanalytical theories, for they are both the observed material and the confirmatory evidence of response to the method. Obviously the trend of patients toward the "well enough" or even "better than well enough" is

4. *Neurotic Mechanisms as Healthy Functions*

Neurosis, too, is part of human nature and has its anthropology.

The split of personality—breakdown as a form of equilibrium—is probably a recently acquired power of human nature, only a few thousand years old. But it is one in a long line of evolutionary developments that are worth briefly reviewing in order to recognize where we are.

If we consider organismic self regulation, the process by which the dominant needs come to the forefront of awareness as they arise, we are struck not only by the wonderful system of specific adjustment, signals, coordination, and subtle judgment that go to maintain the general equilibrium, but also by the devices that serve as cushioners and safety valves to protect the contact boundary. There are blotting-out and hallucinating and dreaming and regarding as-if, and accepting instead-of; and also immobilizing (playing dead), isolating, mechanical trial and error (obsessive redoing), panic flight, and so forth. Man is an organism of great power and efficiency, but also one that can take rough treatment and bad times. The two sides go together: ability leads to adventure and adventure to trouble. Man *has* to be malle-

---

an important factor in the trend of recent theories toward those like our own. In this way psychotherapy is taking over the functions of education, but that is because the customary education—in home, school, university, and church—is increasingly inept. What we would hope for, of course, is that education would take over the functions of psychotherapy.

able. These safety functions all, of course, play a chief role in mental disorders, but they are themselves healthy.

Indeed, without being paradoxical one could say that in the neuroses just these safety functions—of blotting out, distorting, isolating, repeating—that seem so spectacularly "crazy," are working fairly healthily. It is the more respectable functions of orientation and manipulation in the world, especially the social world, that are out of kilter and cannot work. In a finely adjusted whole, the safety devices are made for trouble and continue working while the more usual functions rest for repairs. Or to put it another way, when the orientation is lost and the manipulation is failing, the excitement, the vitality of the organism, expresses itself especially in autism and immobilizing. And so again, if we speak, as we must, of a social or epidemic neurosis, it is not the symptomatic social eccentricities (dictators, wars, incomprehensible art, and the like) that are pathologically important, but the normal knowledge and technique, the average way of life.

The problem of abnormal anthropology is to show how the average way of a culture, or even of the human state, is neurotic and has become so. It is to show what of human nature has been "lost" and, practically, to devise experiments for its recovery. (The therapeutic part of anthropology and sociology is politics; but we see that politics—perhaps fortunately—does not devote itself to this at all.)

In reviewing the steps of evolution leading to modern man and our civilization, therefore, we lay the stress contrary to where it is usually laid: not on the increased power and achievement gained by each step of human development, but on the dangers incurred and the vulnerable points exposed, that then have become pathological in the debacle. The new powers require more complicated integrations, and these have often broken down.

5. Erect Posture, Freedom of Hands and Head

(1) Erect posture developed along with differentiation of the limbs and, ultimately, the fingers. This had great advantages for both orientation and manipulation. A large upright animal gets a long view. Established on broad feet, it can use its hands to get food and tear it, while the head is free, and to handle objects and its own body.

But on the other hand, the head is removed from close perception, and the "close" senses, smell and taste, atrophy somewhat. The mouth and teeth become less useful for manipulation; as such, in an intensely manipulating animal, they tend to pass from felt awareness and response (e.g., there can be a gap between disgust and spontaneous rejection). The jaws and muzzle degenerate —and later will become one of the chief places of rigidity.

In brief, the entire field of the organism and its environment is immensely increased, both in largeness and in minute intricacy; but the closeness of contact is more problematic. And with erect posture comes the need to balance and the danger, so momentous in later psychology, of falling. The back is less flexible, and the head is more isolated from the rest of the body and from the ground.

(II) When the head is freer and less engaged, a sharper stereoscopic vision develops, able to appreciate perspective. The eyes and fingers cooperate in drawing outlines, so that the animal learns to see more shapes and to differentiate objects in his field. By outlining, one differentiates experience into objects. Perspective, discrimination of objects, ability to handle—these greatly increase the number of connections among impressions and the deliberate selectivity among them. The cerebrum grows larger and likely the brightness of consciousness increases. The ability to isolate objects from their situations improves memory and is the beginning of abstracting.

Conversely, there is now likely to be occasional loss of immediacy, of the sense of ready flow with the environment. Images of objects and abstractions about them intervene: the man pauses, with heightened consciousness, for a more deliberate discrimination, but then may forget or be distracted from the goal, and the situation is unfinished. A certain pastness that may or may not be relevant increasingly colors the present.

Finally, one's own body also becomes an object—although later, for this is perceived very "closely."

6. *Tools, Language, Sexual Differentiation, and Society*

(III) When things and other persons have once become outlined and abstracted objects, they can enter into useful deliberate fixed and habitual relations with the self. Permanent tools are developed, along with the *ad hoc* objects that were spontaneous extensions of the limbs; and denotative language is developed along with instinctive situational outcries. Objects are controlled, tools applied to them, and the tools too are objects and may be improved and their use learned and taught. Language too is learned. Spontaneous imitation is deliberately intensified, and the social bond tightens.

But of course the social bond pre-existed; there was communication and the manipulation of the physical and social environment. It is not the use of tools and language that brings persons together or workmen and objects together—they have already been in felt organized contact; the tools and language are convenient differentiations of the contact that exists. The danger that is incurred is this: if the original felt unity weakens, these high-order abstractions—object, person, tool, word—will begin to be taken as the original ground of contact, as if it required some deliberate high-order mental activity in order to get in touch. Thus, interpersonal relations become primarily verbal; or without a suitable tool a workman feels helpless. The differentiation that existed "along with" the underlying organization now exists *instead* of it. Then contact diminishes, speech loses feeling, and behavior loses grace.

(IV) Language and tools combine with the earlier preverbal bonds of sex, nourishment, and imitation, to broaden the scope of society. But such new intricacies may upset the delicately balanced activities that are crucial to the animal's welfare. Consider, for example, how from remote phylogenetic antiquity we have inherited a sexual apparatus exquisitely complicated, involving the senses as excitants, and the motor responses of tumescence, embracing, and intromission, all nicely adjusted toward a mounting climax. (The so-called "adolescent sterility" [Ashley Montagu], the time between the first menstruation and fertility, seems to indicate a period of play and practice.) Besides its advantages of sexual selection and cross-breeding, all this complexity requires at least temporary partnerships: no animal is complete in its own skin. And the strong emotional bonds of lactation, suckling, and fostering care tighten the sociality. Also, in higher phyla, the young animal acquires much of its behavior from imitative learning. Then consider how much depends on what delicate adjustments! Consider that the function of the orgasm (Reich), the essential periodic release of tensions, is bound with the workings of the finely adjusted genital apparatus. It is clear both how important is the social manner of reproduction, and how vulnerable it makes the well-being of the animal.

7. Differentiations of Sensory, Motoric, and Vegetative

(v) Another critical development of fairly remote antiquity has been the separation of the motoric-muscular and sensoric-thought nerve centers. In animals like the dog sensation and motion cannot be much disengaged; this was long ago pointed out by Aristotle, when he said that a dog can reason but it makes only practical syllogisms. The advantages of the looser connection in man are, of course, enormous: the ability to survey, hold back, cogitate, in brief to be deliberate and muscularly hold back the body while letting the senses and thoughts play, along with immediately spontaneously moving in smaller motions of the eyes, hands, vocal cords, etc.

But in neurosis this same division is fateful, for it is seized on in order to prevent spontaneity; and the ultimate practical unity of sense and motion is lost. The deliberation occurs "instead of" rather than "along with": the neurotic loses awareness that the smaller motions are taking place and preparing the larger motions.

(VI) Primitively, the ties of sex, nourishment, and imitation are social but pre-personal: that is, they likely require a sense of the partners not as objects or persons, but merely as what is contacted. But at the stage of toolmaking, language, and other acts of abstraction, the social functions constitute society in our special human sense: a bond among persons. The persons are formed by the social contacts they have, and they identify themselves with the social unity as a whole for their further activity.

There is abstracted from the undifferentiated felt-self a notion, image, behavior, and feeling of the "self" that reflects the other persons. This is the society of the division of labor, in which persons deliberately use one another as tools. It is in this society that taboos and laws develop, bridling the organism in the interest of the superorganism, or better: keeping the persons as persons in interpersonal relationship as well as animals in contact. And this society is, of course, the bearer of what most anthropologists would consider the defining property of mankind: culture, the social inheritance surviving the generations.

The advantages of all this are obvious, and so are the disadvantages. (Here we can begin to speak not of "potential dangers" but of actual surviving troubles.) Controlled by taboos, the imitations become unassimilated introjections, society contained inside the self and ultimately invading the organism; the persons become merely persons *instead of* also animals in contact. The internalized authority lays open the way for institutional exploitation of man by man and of the many by the whole. The division of labor can be pursued in such a way that the work is senseless to the workers and is drudgery. The inherited culture can become a dead weight that one painfully learns, is forced to learn by the duteous elders, yet may never individually use.

8. *Verbal Difficulties in this Exposition*

It is instructive to notice how, in discussing this subject, verbal difficulties begin to arise: "man," "person," "self," "individual," "human animal," "organism" are sometimes interchangeable, sometimes necessary to distinguish. For example, it is deceptive to think of the "individuals" as primitive and combined in social relations, for there is no doubt that the existence of "individuals" comes about as the result of a very complicated society. Again, since it is meaningful to say that it is by organismic self-regulation that one imitates, sympathizes, becomes "independent," and can learn arts and sciences, the expression "animal" contact cannot mean "merely" animal contact. Again, "persons" are reflections of an interpersonal whole, and "personality" is best taken as a formation of the self by a shared social attitude. Yet in an important sense the self, as the system of excitement, orientation, manipulation, and various identifications and alienations, is always original and creative.

These difficulties can, of course, be partly avoided by careful definition and consistent usage—and we try to be as consistent as we can. Yet partly they are inherent in the subject-matter "Man," making himself in different ways. For instance, the early philosophic anthropologists of modern times, in the seventeenth and eighteenth centuries, spoke usually of individuals compacting society; after Rousseau the nineteenth-century sociologists returned to society as primary; and it has been a great merit of psychoanalysis that it has restored these distinct con-

Paul Goodman

cepts to a dynamic interaction. If the theory is often
confusing and ambiguous, it may be that the nature too
is confusing and ambiguous.

9. *Symbols*

We have now brought our history down to the last
several thousand years, since the invention of writing
and reading. Adapting himself to the vast accumulation
of culture, both knowledge and technique, man is edu-
cated in very high abstractions. Abstractions of orientation distant from concernful felt perception: sciences
and systems of science. Abstractions of manipulation distant from muscular participation: systems of production
and exchange and government. He lives in a world of
symbols. He symbolically orients himself as a symbol to
other symbols, and he symbolically manipulates other
symbols. Where there were methods, there is now also
methodology: everything is made the object of hypo-
thesis and experiment, with a certain distance from engagement. This includes society, the taboos, the super-
sensory, the religious hallucinations, and science and
methodology itself, and Man himself. All this has given
an enormous increase in scope and power, for the ability
symbolically to fix what one used to be fully engaged
in allows for a certain creative indifference.

The dangers in it are, unfortunately, not potential but
realized. Symbolic structures—*e.g.*, money or prestige,
or the King's peace, or the advancement of learning—

7 8

become the exclusive end of all activity, in which there is no animal satisfaction and may not even be personal satisfaction; yet apart from animal or at least personal interest there can be no stable intrinsic measure, but only bewilderment and standards that one can never achieve. Thus, economically, a vast mechanism is in operation that does not necessarily produce enough subsistence goods and could indeed, as Percival and Paul Goodman have pointed out in *Communitas*, proceed in almost as high gear without producing any subsistence at all, except that the producers and consumers would all be dead. A worker is crudely or skillfully fitted into a place in this mechanical symbol of plenty, but his work in it does not spring from any pleasure of workmanship or vocation. He may not understand what he is making, nor how, nor for whom. Endless energy is exhausted in the manipulation of marks on paper; rewards are given in kinds of paper, and prestige follows the possession of papers. Politically, in symbolic constitutional structures symbolic representatives indicate the will of the people as expressed in symbolic votes; almost no one, any more, understands what it means to exert political initiative or come to a communal agreement. Emotionally, a few artists catch from real experience symbols of passion and sensory excitement; these symbols are abstracted and stereotyped by commercial imitators; and people make love or adventure according to these norms of glamour. Medical scientists and social workers provide other symbols of emotion and security, and people make love, enjoy recreation and so forth according to prescription. In engineering, control over space, time, and power is symbolically achieved by making it easier to go to less interesting places and easier to get less desirable goods. In pure science, awareness is focused on every detail except the psychosomatic fear and self-conquest of the activity itself, so that, for instance, when there is a question of making certain lethal weapons, the issue debated is whether the need of a country to gain superiority over the enemy outweighs the duty of a scientist to publicize his findings; but the simpler reactions of compassion, flight, defiance are not operative at all.

In these conditions it is not surprising that persons toy with the sadomasochism of dictatorships and wars, where there is at least control of man by man instead of by symbols, and where there is suffering in the flesh.

10. *Neurotic Split*

So finally we come to a very recent acquisition of mankind, the neurotically split personality as a means of achieving equilibrium. Faced with a chronic threat to any functioning at all, the organism falls back on its safety devices of blotting-out, hallucination, displacement, isolation, flight, regression; and man essays to make "living on his nerves" a new evolutionary achievement.

In the early stages there were developments that the healthy organism could each time merge into a new integrated whole. But now it is as if neurotics went back and singled out the vulnerable points of the past development of the race: the task is not to integrate erect posture into animal life, but to act on the one hand as if the head stood in the air by itself and on the other hand as if there were no erect posture or no head at all; and so with the other developments. The potential "dangers" have become factual symptoms: contactlessness, isolation, fear of falling, impotence, inferiority, verbalizing, and affectlessness.

It remains to be seen whether or not this neurotic turn is a viable destiny for our species.

11. *Golden Age, Civilization, and Introjections*

We have been generally defining the neurotic adjustments here as those which employ the new power "instead of" the previous nature, which is repressed, rather than "along with" it, in a new integration. The repressed unused natures then tend to return as Images of the Golden Age, or Paradise; or as theories of the Happy Primitive. We can see how great poets, like Homer and Shakespeare, devoted themselves to glorifying precisely the virtues of the previous era, as if it were their chief function to keep people from forgetting what it used to be to be a man.

And at best, indeed, the conditions of advancing civilized life seem to make important powers of human nature not only neurotically unused but rationally unusable. Civil security and technical plenty, for instance, are not very appropriate to an animal that hunts and perhaps needs the excitement of hunting to enliven its full powers. It is not surprising if such an animal should often complicate quite irrelevant needs—*e.g.*, sexuality—with danger and hunting, in order to rouse excitement.

Further, it is likely that there is at present an irreconcilable conflict between quite desirable social harmony and quite desirable individual expression. If we are in such a transitional stage toward a tighter sociality, then there will be in individuals many social traits that must appear as unassimilable introjections, neurotic and inferior to the rival individual claims. Our heroic ethical standards (which come from the inspiriting dreams of creative artists) certainly tend to look backward to the more animal, sexual, personal, valorous, honorable, etc.; our behavior is quite otherwise and lacks excitement.

On the other hand, it is also likely (even if the different likelihoods are contradictory) that these "irreconcilable" conflicts have always been, not only at present, the human condition; and that the attendant suffering and motion toward an unknown solution are the grounds of human excitement.

12. *Conclusion*

However it is, "human nature" is a potentiality. It can be known only as it has been actualized in achievement and history, and as it makes itself today.

The question may quite seriously be asked, By what criterion does one prefer to regard "human nature" as what is actual in the spontaneity of children, in the works of heroes, the culture of classic eras, the community of simple folk, the feeling of lovers, the sharp awareness and miraculous skill of some people in emergencies? Neurosis is also a response of human nature and is now epidemic and normal, and perhaps has a viable social future.

We cannot answer the question. But a medical psychologist proceeds according to three criteria: (1) the health of the body, known by a definite standard, (2) the progress of the patient toward helping himself, and (3) the elasticity of the figure/background formation.

Dr. Walter Kempler

Experiential Family Therapy

Experiential family therapy is a psychotherapeutic approach to the treatment of emotionally disturbed individuals within the framework of the family. Its core is experiential exploration of the "what and how" of "I and thou" in the "here-and-now." A fundamental of such an approach is the acceptance of the vital importance of the immediate, the present, the whole, not to exclude perspective but to establish a central point to which that perspective can be related.

The family framework, has, of course, always been implicitly and explicitly recognized, as has, in remoter context, the social, economic, ethnic, and national status of the individual. But many therapists have assumed until recently that treatment could proceed only—or at least more beneficially—with a temporary physical divorce of the patient from his familial surroundings during the therapeutic interviews.

Individual therapy had and has its subjective advantages; however, in many instances these are overbalanced by the benefits of an approach that brings together the family group with the therapist. Therapeutic sessions are inevitably artificial in arrangement and atmosphere. Individual sessions dignify the patient with peculiar importance, exemplified by the entire attention of the therapist, while at the same time removing him from the ordinary actions and counter-actions of his daily life. The few hours of the week spent with the psychiatrist are far outweighed, in duration at least, by the many hours spent with the family. It is the case of the sand in *Alice:*

> "If seven maids with seven mops
> Swept it for half a year,
> Do you suppose," the Walrus said,
> "That they could get it clear?"
> "I doubt it," said the Carpenter,
> And shed a bitter tear.

Just too much sand and not enough mops.

Experiential family therapy is particularly well suited to individuals who are captive to family, whether by virtue of age (children) or inclination (adults who identify their problems as interpersonal). However, it is not limited to these categories, but has been used successfully in treatment of individuals, couples, and groups whose needs have not been so manifest. No diagnostic classification is contraindicated, and family participants include many who would otherwise never have seen a psychotherapist.

Most of us who have begun to approach psychotherapy within the context of the family unit rather than by following the traditional method of separating an individual from his intimate environment have come to it by way of the family who presents us with a disturbed child as the identified patient. The success of the family technique in these instances led to an exploration of other applications for the "family" approach to treatment. Any two persons who feel strongly about preserving a relationship and who blame the existence or course of that relationship for their personal discomforts may be considered eligible; that is, childless couples need not be deprived.

I have been confronted by patients whose complaints were of interpersonal rather than intrapsychic discomfort. By the end of the interview, it was apparent that the individual's personality was what we typically call a character disorder with little anxiety or capacity for introspection. Psychiatric literature generally reports such individuals as difficult to treat, and personal experience has tended to confirm this. With the concept of family pathology, I have been able to accept these patients' starting point of an interpersonal rather than an intrapersonal construction of their problems, and have suggested that the irritant party, usually a spouse, be included, since the problem is posed as existing between two people. (It would not be reasonable to send one lung to one hospital and the other to another for treatment of pneumonia.) Once resistance to this is acknowledged as the therapist's rather than the patient's, a profitable beginning has been made.

The approach is an experiential or phenomenological one characterized by exploration, experiment, and spontaneity. By spontaneity I mean allowing subsurface material to emerge whenever possible from myself and the people I sit with. It means encouraging an atmosphere in which the underlying flow of affect toward or away from each other is welcomed as part of our verbal exchange. I encourage this atmosphere by doing it, being it, and sometimes by exploring verbally my difficulty in doing it; never by talking about (broadcasting or announcing) this desired atmosphere. In exploring and experimenting, no topic is taboo from our right to toy with it, tease it apart, or "try it on for size." However, spontaneity is not license for manifest irrelevances or abstract discussion, no matter how tempting; these are, of course, resistances on the part of the therapist or the patient. The approach is predicated on the assumption that in the room, within the accepted setting, the family members and the therapist have needs that will emerge. These needs may come out as thoughts fully or partially expressed, feelings subtly indicated or vehemently vented, changes of posture, gesticulations, or perhaps fantasies that develop in the mind of the individual and are not shared with the group.

To the expression of these needs, adequate or, more likely, halting reactions occur: comfort, antagonism, worry, detachment, horror, disgust, resentment, indifference, pleasure, and so on, endlessly. Sensitivity to these evidences of human interaction is encouraged, and attention is directed to the use to which awareness of them is put. This applies to therapist and patient alike. If I become aware of being bored, I will consider my boredom and most likely mention it. If I get the idea that all the verbiage spoken by one of the group to another could be summarized in the statement, "I want your unqualified approval of my behavior," I may suggest that this member experiment by trying out this statement with the other person.

This therapy is kept vital by constant attention to our differences. Awareness in this sense always includes who is doing what to whom and how it is perceived by others. Awareness means action. When an active (total behavioral response, not merely verbal agreement or abstract discussion) response is absent, I ask, as the lighthouse keeper did who awoke when his light failed, "What wasn't that?" The inactive response then comes to the foreground. I judge the effectiveness of what I do by direct observation of altered behavior and peripheral cue comments of outside experiences. If there is a discrepancy between the two, I am likely to comment on it. If behavior is being altered merely to please me and I sense this, I will introduce my thought for their perusal. If I am not aware of this, then so be it, until such time as the resentment they are likely to feel comes to the awareness of one or both of us. Then we will attend to it. I say likely rather than inevitably since sometimes their altered behavior, although motivated primarily by a desire to please, is sufficiently rewarding to preclude any concern with revenge. A goal I have for others is behavior predicated on pleasing themselves. This may or may not be achieved. The decision does not rest with me.

My aim is to utilize these family sessions as a meaningful experience and to encourage the participants to engage themselves likewise, not as spectators or aloof commentators, but as vitally concerned combatants. It is still a process of pointing up and ferreting out resistances, as we have traditionally formulated, but the orientation here considers the patients as resisting awareness of themselves and involvement in their current world, wherever they may find themselves.

I am interested in coming to know the persons I am with. To this end I am interested primarily in the what and how of their behavior; my concern with the verbal content is almost exclusively in this perspective. The verbal content or subject matter per se is for me the launching equipment to be jettisoned as soon as possible in favor of a free flight of self-awareness and of self-expression, literally, direct expression of self in the atmosphere of another. By responding to the "what and how," a more intense and vital interaction ensues. This is something that not all people can accept at all times. I find myself diluting the intensity by concentrating on verbalizations when my patient reveals to me as a total response, not just verbally, that he cannot tolerate the intensity. This may become the next thing we discuss.

In such a give-and-take, an exploration of the differences in our perceptions of ourselves and others and an examination of what we do or do not do with this awareness takes place. But it does not take place in the isolation of introspection. It occurs in an atmosphere of human, familial, and immediate concern that makes a crucial contribution to movement in therapy.

In terms of the familiar concept of transference, this technique of family group therapy does not foster regressive phenomena in relation to the therapist, only for the patient to be confronted at some later "suitable" time with the reality of who the therapist is and what he is as distinguished from the images projected upon him. Experiential family group therapy presents a constant exposure of transference phenomena whenever experienced in the psychotherapy sessions. From the outset I discourage the fabrication of a stylized or stereotyped image labeled "therapist" or "doctor." "I am whatever I happen to be" is, of course, an oversimplification, but it suggests rough approximation with a status I think essential to this therapy. The family group not only has the opportunity to know this, but should any of them at any point contaminate my identity with, for instance, a projection of a parent as that parent appeared to them earlier in life, this would become the focus of my attention.

Members of the group have the same privilege of offering or insisting upon what they feel is a more accurate personal image. In this atmosphere the therapist often feels most keenly the therapeutic aspects of the experience. By being, so nearly as possible, a total person, rather than by playing the role of therapist, the atmosphere encourages all members to participate more fully as total personalities. Such resistances to functioning as may occur in this atmosphere may also become the focus of attention in our group.

At this point, or perhaps earlier, the question may be raised: Are such techniques a short cut? If a short cut means bypassing some of the unpleasant moments that seem to me inherent in developing awareness and change, the answer is no. If it means abbreviating the number of hours in treatment, the answer is yes.

The conjoint family therapy structure further contributes to this in several ways. First, it identifies the patient as the family rather than any single member of it. This modification of structure immediately confronts many resistances other than that of the one who has been identified as the patient. In one family the father, a policeman, brought in his "delinquent" son, identifying the boy as the patient. The essence of the father's attitude toward his son was: I don't want you to be a delinquent and I try to prevent it by showing you criminals so you can see what they are and how they have become so; and by insisting you do not break rules and then overlooking it when you do. When this attitude was examined in the family sessions, all family members assisted in deterring this delinquent-provoking behavior. Had I seen the boy alone, with the family continuing to identify the problem as solely that of the son's behavior, this hidden domestic pressure would have been a tremendous force in thwarting any efforts the boy and I could make by ourselves.

A second way in which family therapy works to shorten the course of behavioral change is when one member of the family begins to modify self-defeating behavior. Often, another family member, fearful of change or "needing" the other member's self-defeating behavior, resists this change, and when it happens within the purview of the group, it immediately commands attention. In individual therapy these manipulations by others often go unnoticed by the patient (and consequently the therapist) for long periods.

A third way in which family therapy favorably affects the course of psychotherapy is in the empathic response. To witness another member of the family exposing, for instance, some fear or anxiety, in preference to a defensive pose of bravado, usually elicits a new response from the observer. The others suddenly see through the defensiveness and respond with compassion and understanding as they feel less threatened. Another important contribution is the developing awareness by momentarily silent members that they are not the sole cause of each others' problems. As projections are lifted off spouses and children, all members have greater freedom to seek new ways of responding. It provides a rapid method for disentangling interlocking psychopathology.

I have seen patients alter in a manner they and those around them considered more satisfactory when they changed from one therapist to another, both of whom I have felt to be competent. In part, this may be due to different therapists' evoking different responses, not necessarily through the application of differing techniques but simply by the impingement of their differing personalities. Family members have the effect both of serving as unique stimuli to the patient and responding uniquely to the patient's behavior.

When a family member calls for an appointment and identifies a problem as familial or primarily involving another family member, I press hard to have the other members join in the initial interview. If a child is involved, the entire family is asked to come in. During the course of family therapy, individual sessions are avoided. From experience I find individual sessions unnecessary, manipulative, and, most of all, tending to be destructive for the requesting member. When confronted with the most popular mechanism, "I have something to say that I can't say in front of the others," in keeping with this approach, I suggest that they simply make this statement to "the others" during the session. These "secret data," important as the implications are, can be left unstressed, and attention drawn to what the protagonist is doing and what responses the others make to this stimulus. Again, the "what and how" of the current behavior pre-empts the verbal content.

Response to my suggestion is rarely compliance; more likely an attempt at evasion is made: "But it's you I want to say it to." To my, "Why me?" they may answer, "Because you would understand and they won't." "Tell this to them." If they answer, "I can't," I retort, "Then tell *that* to them." If the point is reached where I get a flat, "No!" I stop pressing and wait for subsequent phenomena, either a comment from a family member about what has happened or a shifting of the focus of attention to some other matter. This is an important moment in this type of therapy. It would be easy to yield to temptation and utilize this opportunity for all kinds of explanations and interpretations, such as: this individual has put me in the same position as the family members —of being unable to understand him—because I do not comply with his request; or, he has had a verbal battle with me, and in the process of coming to me for help has refused that help in order to win the battle of the moment. But not only would this be fruitless, it would also thwart his opportunity to evaluate the exchange on his own terms, at his own speed, as well as interfering with the chance for other members of the family to respond to the maneuver. The only interjection I might make at this point would be an observation on some non-verbal expression in the room, such as a rejecting grimace on the part of another member during the exchange.

The relevance of this approach is that this family has come to me for help. One member says he has something to say to me—that is, that I am the focus of his attention. It is apparent to me that his world does not really include me but uses me merely as rescuer in an attempt to avoid experiencing something with the other members who are the primary figures in his life at the moment. This person is trying to tell the others that he is unable to talk to them. It seems easier for many of us to tell a stranger that we like him than to tell an intimate that we do not like him. This becomes the crucial observation. As part of the therapeutic technique I continue to refuse to accept a positive comment to me as a substitute for a negative one to a primary person in the individual's life.

Sometimes the would-be escapist complies, turning

to another family member and saying, "I don't really expect you to understand me. You never do. You always twist things around." To this the other member responds with, "I don't know what in hell you're talking about. You are the one who doesn't understand, not me." I wait. The principals are involved and I now retire, to return at the next impasse. I want the first party to point out the live demonstration by the second of what he was saying. I want the second to say more about his anger toward the first. I want them to do this for themselves. So I wait. What is likely to happen is that the first reverts back to his original posture and either looks helplessly at me or sits dejectedly staring at the floor. The second also sits silently. Now I may re-enter and have my say. To the first member: "Your partner proves your point and you respond by collapsing and fleeing." And to the second member: "You seemed so angry." Now I wait and see who does what to whom next and how it is done. I hope that one of them will respond to my comments and begin a fruitful exchange with the other. Should they start to speak to me instead, I will again encourage, in some way, their self-awareness and involvement with each other.

It is difficult to spell out what I would specifically say or do. It depends on what I sense would be appropriate to everyone's needs as I know them at that moment, including my own. I am unable to describe all the variables that comprise my intuitive behavior. The principles enunciated in this paper are admittedly primitive and crude, but they are the only way I know at present to begin.

Structure and technique are often overlapping. Three principles I use in the structuring of interviews are certainly to be considered aspects of the technique, and the category in which they may be placed depends solely on application. If they are a precondition of the interview, we can call them structure; if they are part of the verbal interplay, they become aspects of technique. For me they were aspects of technique originally but have now become a part of structure in most instances; I have eliminated them as operational obstacles by confronting them directly when they occur. These three principles are: no interruptions, no questions, no gossip. Interruptions, if not picked up by other members of the group, are pointed out by me. I say, "You interrupted," and to the others, "You permitted the interruption." Those interrupted are no less responsible than those who do the interrupting. When it persists, I point out that interruptions are inefficient, wasteful, and a destructive mechanism better excluded. Should they continue, I become a principal and proclaim, often with considerable effect, that they have come to me for help and persistently ignore what help I can offer.

Questions are communication media for obtaining information. Socially they are used for many other purposes, for, among other things, establishing superficial and avoiding more personal contact. It is the rare exemplar who will not give a person the time of day. The person can pick a category ("What do you think of the weather?") without making a commitment or assuming any responsibility. But on the assumption that an individual comes to treatment seeking knowledge of himself, the questions have little place. On rare occasions a point of information is legitimately sought but more often questioning is a maneuver to obscure or evade. Whatever words the therapist actually employs, questions are met with a request like, "Please convert that into a statement starting with the word 'I.' "

Gossiping describes any remark made *about* rather than *to* the other person. It is a popular method of escape from immediate pressure. Consonant with the technique, if a remark is directed to the therapist about another member of the family, the therapist urges that it be redirected to the involved subject. Should the gossiper refuse, the therapist suggests the refusal itself be directed to the other member.

Clearly, the tendency of both patient and therapist is to escape from the "here-and-now" experience. Therapists know the patients' techniques well, and readily detect and label them as resistances. We are less familiar with our own. Common resistances used by therapists are immersion in historical data; raising "why" questions, which send both patient and therapist scurrying off into the world of abstract thought; and encouraging exploration of circumstances that are not immediate and are of questionable theoretical pertinence.

The alacrity with which patients bring out samples from their vast storehouses of memories reveal their feeling of safety with these samples and preference for living in this world of talking-aboutness. It is not so easy to elicit their responses to the here and now, including their feelings toward the therapist and what is going on. A preference for "talking about" material from earlier in the same session has been observed to represent avoidance of more painful immediate material.

Here is what happened at the start of a first interview with a mother, father, and their two daughters aged eight and fourteen. There was no history elicited. Whatever it was, it would be reflected in their current behavior, and this was enough; there was no need to go into the past. The only contact and information I had prior to this interview was a call from the mother who complained about the behavior of the fourteen-year-old daughter, expressing the fear that she was becoming a "juvenile delinquent," citing stealing the family car, doing poor schoolwork, ditching school, and going with the wrong crowd of kids who were having wild parties at which petting was the obvious and primary activity. The mother wanted an appointment to tell me more before I saw the daughter. I assured her that it would not be necessary to prime me ahead of time and offered an appointment time when *all* members of the family could come together.

The family looked conventional enough. The fourteen-year-old's rather disheveled appearance was in contrast to the rest of the family's neat attire. The mother was particularly well groomed, and sat alert, upright, and attentive. The father's face was expressionless. The eight-year-old smiled at me. The fourteen-year-old slouched in her chair, looking off into the distance. The mother alternately glanced at the fourteen-year-old and at me. No one spoke. The pressure was clearly mounting in the mother, and it was apparent that the entire family supported her wish to be the spokesman. Finally, she opened with, "As I told you on the phone, we're having sort of a problem with our daughter. I don't know quite where to begin." There was a silence.

"I don't know where to begin either," I said.

"Something happened to Milly [as I shall call her] in the seventh grade that I think is important for her to tell you about."

She was gossiping to me about her daughter, so I remarked, "Perhaps this is something you could discuss with Milly herself."

She turned to the girl. "Milly, why don't you tell the doctor about the incident in the seventh grade?"

Milly replied to this with a grunt and a negative head-shake. The mother persisted, repeating the question, adding, "I think it's very important. Why don't you tell the doctor?" The mother's intent smile was slightly strained; she looked at me, probably for encouragement, and then went back to prodding Milly to reveal what had happened. After several fruitless tries, I made two observations to the mother. I remarked that she was trying to get her daughter to talk about herself when she, the mother, was apparently unwilling to reveal herself; that although she was speaking, she was not speaking of herself or what she wanted, but instead had put the responsibility on the daughter by way of the repeated question, which kept herself free of direct involvement. I also noted aloud that she had apparently had not heard her daughter refuse, since she kept repeating the same question.

The mother quickly responded, "Oh, no. You misunderstand, Doctor. She knew what I meant. We communicate with each other very well. She knows exactly how I feel and I know how she feels, and we are able to talk together freely all the time." Then she reflected a moment and said, "I didn't mean to put her on the spot; I just thought it important that she tell you about the incident. Well, I suppose I could talk about myself."

I began to feel that the mother was playing a game of I've-got-a-secret in collaboration with her daughter. She would not reveal something she felt was important; neither would Milly. What they were doing to each other and to me at the moment was of greater interest than the ostensible purpose of the session. I waited in the silence for the next move; no one else in the family seemed to have any inclination to say anything.

The mother became restive in her chair and somewhat faltering in her speech as she said, "I . . . I guess I could say some things about myself. I don't know just where to begin. I don't know what you want me to talk about. I wasn't prepared to talk about myself. My mind was on Milly and her problems. It didn't occur to me to talk about myself. . . ." I alluded to her behavior, mentioning her restlessness and the hesitancy in her speech, and suggested that she appeared uncomfortable. "I *am* uncomfortable," she said.

Moving from her verbal communication to her total communication, I suggested she discuss her discomfort. "I suppose I hesitate to speak about myself in front of the children. It's rather uncomfortable. Probably I want them to see me as strong and knowing what I'm doing." She laughed nervously. This was gossiping, and her statement was not really for all of us. Since she was speaking of her feelings in relation to her children, I suggested she direct her comments to them. She looked somewhat startled, turned to the fourteen-year-old, stared at her for a moment, and burst into tears. After her crying had subsided, she said to Milly, "I guess I don't want you to know how inadequate I feel as a mother. I've even thought now and then that you might be better off if you had a mother who knew what she was doing. I feel so inadequate. I don't know why I try so hard to keep this from you. I guess I'm afraid you won't have any respect for me." Mother and daughter confronted each other in searching silence. The mother went on, "This must be why I expect so much from you. If you become the perfect daughter, you reassure me that I'm a good mother. That must be why I expect so much." By now Milly was also crying. Father and the eight-year-old sat quietly.

The mother kept on talking. She spoke to Milly about recent incidents in which conflict between them had been most painful for the mother. As she went on her tone and demeanor gradually shifted from the kindly parent to the didactic lecturer. The content changed from admission of her own inadequacy to complaints of her daughter's shortcomings and the need for both of them to turn over a new leaf. Milly stopped crying. Father and the eight-year-old still sat silent and motionless. I did not.

When making observations during an interaction, it is often useful to make comparable comments to both parties, giving each the opportunity to hear an observer's view of their separate behaviors, so I mentioned to the mother the change in her attitude and the content of what she was saying, and observed to the daughter that she had stopped crying and had turned away again to stare blankly into space without answering her mother. Milly looked at me and exclaimed exasperatedly, "She does this all the time." This was gossiping, so I suggested she tell this to her mother, further suggesting that she comment to her on how she felt about this. This was an attempt on my part to get her to make verbal the exasperation so evident in her expression. Milly complied to the extent that she said wryly to her mother, "You know you do this all the time."

The mother's response was to override her daughter's comment with another lecture beginning with a typical dismissal comment: "Yes, but . . ." I remarked to the mother that she was lecturing again and had ignored her daughter's words. The mother looked perplexed, saying, "I must do this all the time. I've never been conscious of it before. I don't know what to do about it though; I can't seem to stop it." I suggested she tell this to Milly. She did. Milly answered, "Why don't you just listen to me once in a while? When you come into my room and I ask you to leave, you always refuse. Why don't you just go out?"

Before I had time to interrupt—and it would have been an interruption—to suggest to Milly that she convert her questions into more meaningful statements about her wishes and feelings, the mother answered, "I can't do that. I have to finish what I'm saying first. Or do I? Maybe I'm just lecturing there, too." The mother looked thoughtful, and then she and Milly smiled at each other.

I, too, felt pleased. I felt that a point of healthy contact had been made between them which they had acknowledged. For me it represented a point of closure, and I now became aware of all four members again.

There was another silence, and I found myself wondering where the father stood in all this, so I turned to him: "You haven't said a word." He smiled and answered, "I never say much." The mother remarked to me, "He's never said much. It's only recently that he's begun to participate in the family at all. Milly said the other day that it has been only lately that she really felt she had a father." Milly nodded confirmation. The father remained impassive. I was aware that the mother was being his spokesman and he was permitting it, but I chose to focus on a softer issue at this time: the content of the mother's statement. I asked him whether he had been aware of this reaction from his daughter. "No, this is the first I've heard of it, although I know I haven't been too close to the rest of the family. It's getting better now, I believe."

The mother hastened to agree with him. Now I pointed out to the mother her part as spokesman for the father, and to the father his passive acceptance of this. The mother smiled and said to me, "I'm the talker and will speak for anybody who will let me. He doesn't mind." Her husband nodded, saying, "It's all right with me." There was no apparent conflict here, at least not at the moment. My thoughts moved to Milly's relationship with her father and I pointed out to him that he hadn't responded directly to her observation. He began to repeat that he was now more involved with the family. "I understand," I said, "but I'm wondering what you felt when you heard what your daughter said."

He looked puzzled at first. "I suppose I feel sorry."

"You suppose?"

After a moment he said, "No, I *am* sorry she feels this way." He had now clarified his current sentiments toward Milly, had permitted himself to examine them, but telling them to me was gossip. I suggested he state them directly to her. He turned to Milly. "I'm sorry you felt this way. I suppose I knew it, but just didn't want to see it. As your mother says, I've been around a lot more lately, and I'm going to try to be around even more. Okay?" Milly nodded.

The mother smiled and said to me, "That's a lot of talking for him." Before having her direct her remark to its appropriate target, I asked her how she felt about his unusual loquacity. "I like it," she said to him.

At the conclusion of the hour, as they were leaving, the mother said to me cheerfully, "I boasted how well we talked to each other, but we've probably talked more to each other in this hour than in the past couple of years."

This family terminated treatment after six weekly interviews. During that time the daughter's acting out had stopped and the entire family agreed that Milly's behavior and relationship with the family had changed remarkably for the better; the eight-year-old participated actively in parts of two sessions, appeared quite healthy, and identified mildly with her older sister in condemning the mother's dominance. ("When I ask you to help me with one arithmetic problem, you do all of them for me.") Mother's steamrolling and discussion of Father's seeming excessive sensitivity and tendency to withdraw from the family were the two central themes of our six sessions, although many other aspects of child and parental and therapist behavior had our attention.

This family was seen about a year ago. I called recently to inquire about their current status. The mother was the only one home. The following is an excerpt from the conversation:

THERAPIST: I'm wondering if you would venture an opinion on the sessions that we had. Do you feel they were of any help?

MOTHER: I would say yes, but it was too superficial, you know, just six sessions, when you have chronic behavior that's been going on for thirty years. What are six hours? It almost just scratches so lightly.

THERAPIST: Yes, well, that is what I am trying to evaluate. I am also wondering about the children; do you think it was of any benefit to them, or to the family in general?

MOTHER: I think it helped Milly quite a bit. Before we went to you, Milly thought she was some sort of delinquent kid, you know, and I think after our experience with you she realized more that she was part of a group and there was a mother who was a steamroller and so maybe she wasn't this scary kid she thought she was. That was of great value.

THERAPIST: One of the things I recall that we talked about in our meetings was some of the relationship, or lack of relationship, between Milly and her father. I'm wondering if since that time there has been any change in that? I recall your revealing for the first time a statement Milly made to you that she felt like sometimes she really didn't have a father.

MOTHER: Well, now, apparently there have been tremendous changes. At this point I would say that Milly and her Dad have a lovely loving relationship and that they are very important to each other, and there's a great deal of interaction, and your comments sound like they are almost not the same two people. I have more respect for my husband, which may be related.

This is not a case report of a successful analysis of an entire family in a single hour or in six hours using the techniques of experiential family therapy. But it describes a not atypical initial visit and is submitted mainly to transmit some flavor of the approach. This paper presents an approach to psychotherapy with the structure of the family. The goal is fuller awareness of self in the world with others, with the implicit corollary that, coupled with the inherent drive in all of us for a more satisfying and efficient existence, achievement of this end is possible.

The approach is oriented to an exploration of the resistances to experience within the psychotherapy session itself. Gossiping, interrupting, and questioning are popular diversionary tactics used by patients. Seeking historical data and genetic derivatives are common diversions from the therapeutic goal employed by the therapist.

Paul Goodman

Growing Up

My daughter is stricken with polio and her legs are seriously involved, but I want her to get out of bed and walking in a few days. I am set on this one thought and nothing else will allay my hope and fear.

At the hospital, however, the doctor speaks of transfer, after the acute stage, to another hospital for rehabilitation. He mentions months of time and wearing braces, or even sitting in a wheel chair. I reject these ideas violently and hate the man who utters them. I will not discuss the hospitals he names and their various advantages.

A few days later, when she is not making progress satisfactory to me, I am sure she is not getting the right treatment at the hospital where in fact she is. I now fear that she may not ultimately—in several months—fully recover. So I try frantically to have her at once removed to another hospital. But there are obstacles; she does not yet meet the criteria for discharge and readmission. I refuse to accept the obstacles. I am now set with great determination on this new thought, the other hospital, the very idea I had so recently violently rejected.

I work hard at this, and succeed; whereas with my previous hope and fear I could do nothing.

This is an important sequence of feelings. By cumulative repetitions of it we grow up, for better or worse. Let me spell it out.

1. Our primary wish cannot be worked at and is intolerably anxious. Therefore, it slips away and we push it away.

2. We accept the defeat of our wish by making the very content of its defeat the central goal of our second striving.

3. The new goal is pettier. It is not desirable in itself, but good in the circumstances, a lesser evil.

4. We do not forgive the person in authority who thwarted our dear first wish. We try to escape from him.

5. But his painful idea persists and becomes central.

6. We ourselves betray our first wish, no longer willing it single-mindedly. But we frantically combine elements of it with the idea that defeated it.

7. The new combination has now become our "own" wish; we work hard at it, and boast of any success we achieve.

8. The primary wish survives in isolation, as a distant hope, exempt from the test of present reality.

9. We learn a new adjustment to reality and go on.

Betraying one's wish and embracing the content that defeated it occurs inevitably in the conditions that are prevalent in early life. In the present case, these conditions have reoccurred:

I am ignorant in the situation and cannot take practical steps of my own, so I am awed by an authority. He does not win my trust, respect, or affection, and I want to defy him, rebel against him, and take over on my own. But I am afraid of disapproval and punishment, and I cannot cope with the consequences without him. I cannot assume responsibility.

He is almost like a successful rival who has unworthily won authority in the hospital. I doubt his ultimate skill and daring, and have more secret confidence in my own. It seems to me that he disposes of my daughter (and me) without the earnest attention that I would give. He really does not care.

But my antagonist is strong, and my own wish is ambivalent and weak. Reconsider it: I want my daughter to get up and walk quickly. If this were a simple desire, the alternative—of a slow and perhaps imperfect recovery—would *not* seem like an antagonist, but like a hard possible reality, in which to be patient, prudent, determined, and hopeful of the best. Instead, the wish was panicky as if I myself were attacked. The idea of my daughter crippled endangers my image of myself: nothing practical can follow from such a fantasy.

Certainly the first wish does not *center* in the girl and

her welfare. My compulsive denying of her threatening fact is not far from denying her existence: "*You* have no right to be in danger. Be as I need or don't bother me."

Children are inevitably caught in this kind of situation. Powerless and ignorant, they are subject to demands by big and knowing authorities who do not win their trust and assent, but whom they cannot quit and against whom they cannot rebel. Matters become worse when the satisfaction of many of the child's desires, whether narcissistic, erotic, or ambitious, is further made impossible by fear, guilt, shame, and deprivation. The child is soon out of touch with what he needs, and he is shaky even about what he thinks he wants. Therefore, in a crisis he easily gives up the content of his own wish and identifies with the wishes of his authorities. He is then safe, blameless, and even boastful.

As an adult I am not quite so powerless. I rally and draw on new real resources and so do not altogether repress my original wish. Since I distrust the authority in the hospital, I consult a physician from among my friends. He suggests various hospitals and although perforce I give up my literal wish, I judge in terms of the same criteria of speedy and complete recovery, and I make a choice. On inquiry I find that the care that she has been getting is indeed all that can be done at this stage (according to present knowledge), so I am more reconciled to the physician-in-charge and I apologize to him.

Within the limits of prudence, I venture to exert my own two-bits of therapeutic wisdom. I see that my daughter is in a panic of fear, and this I can alleviate. I give myself to all-day visits, I somewhat calm her fears and lighten the long hours. And since action leads to feeling and feeling to understanding, I now have her as a real object of affection, and I see the whole matter in perspective and more practically.

Tangentially, I engage in a good deal of bitter griping to my friends about big hospitals, etc. This energizes political and social ideas of mine.

By these means I cannot at all resolve the problem, but I can diminish my anxiety and unlike a child, I can keep the matter out of repression. A child can adjust to "reality" only by repression and identification. But a creative adjustment can find new truth and excitement in the problem itself. New life springs from the collapse of the *status quo*. One draws on new resources, of compassion to remedy, of study and invention to make prosper, of patience to endure.

My own behavior falls midway between the childish adjustment and the creative adjustment. I have a kind of patience, but it is nagging and worrying. I can act, but erratically and with unnecessary friction. My anxiety is not allayed because I am attached to myself in the past and I do not embrace the faith that destiny is providence. Yet I am able to diminish my guilt and resentment by coming, in many small ways, closer into contact with the situation, so my anxiety is manageable.

Joseph Schlichter

Movement Therapy

We have been pushing, locked against each other, driving hard with our legs, shoulder to shoulder. Our grunting and shortened breathing turn to roaring challenges. I grasp my throat, straining for air, opening my mouth and moving my lips without sound—noiseless words and screams. My eyes bulge pleadingly and blink in panic. A sound blurts from my mouth and I scramble-fumble into a corner. Falling . . . crouching . . . sobbing . . . I don't know? I don't know! I don't know!!! I can't scream. I can't breathe.

I beat and windmill my arms around, clenching fists and eyes, hunched back and squeezed-together thighs. My feet run away from me. I trip. Grimace. They copy what I do—those mirrors: multifaceted; multishaped. Coney Island. They keep doing it. The nerve of the asses. Their screams, curses, choking grunts don't fit their movements. I've got to stop this noise. My hands can't block it out. I can't stand this shit. I can't stand this. Wilder and more frantic now. I won't make sounds. Their noise is my thermometer. My throat! My throat! The floor is tilting. Stop it! Stop it! My eyes are cold. They are all spinning and yelling at me. I see myself falling. It doesn't hurt. I can't breathe, I can't breathe, I can't stand it. I need that wall. Tears. I hate this. You know I hate this, you son of a bitch. You have my wrists and hold them doggedly. I see our struggle. We are rolling around the floor. Please let me go! I cajole. I threaten . . . me . . . you . . . I try to hit you. More struggling. I go limp; it doesn't work. I pretend to give up; it doesn't work. I jerk hard! I'll *kill* the bastard. You're too fast for my biting. My curses float in my ear. I give up.

You kiss me gently on the cheek and turn my face. You smack me and turn my face. Ooooooooooo! Kisses on my cheek; I turn the other. You smack the cheek. I turn my other. I smack your cheek; you turn the other. I kiss your-my cheek. Over and over and under and on top and . . . Again. . . .

It is all too slow. Or is it too fast? Sobbing. No, no, I don't, I didn't mean to do it, Mommy, I didn't do it, no, no. I collapse. . . . My drunken mother choking my aunt in front of me because of something I said.

My glib tongue is cut off; lip service is silenced. Movement is the medium.

Our American taboos say little or no touching. If we can't touch, I can't make real: I like you; I am angry with us; I need comforting; I love you-me.

I leap and stamp across the room. My fists are clenched; they pump up and down. I see only the floor. Later, doing the same thing another way, I smack myself in the face: right side, left side, right side, left side, over and over until I burst into tears. . . . Minutes. . . . I muster myself up. I scold and yell at the women in the room, forcing them down on the floor, sweeping them into one pile. Finally, I refuse to do anything. All I can be is destructive. I will not, I cannot do anything to help the pile of sprawled women. I can't speak to them. . . . Minutes. . . . I rouse everyone to join hands in a circle and sway. We are quietly together, touching side by side, arms linked around the waist. Somehow, I am going somewhere. Just where, who knows yet?

We mirror, echo, and reverse. These might be called repetition, distortion, and opposition or synonyms, homonyms, and antonyms if you like. The methods melt into each other. To mirror is to copy as exactly as is possible what you see someone else doing in movement. When I mirror I don't invade—I just let you be. To echo is to distort another's or your own movement. Echoing is exaggeration. It is going further with it, seeing where it goes and where it comes from for yourself and only yourself. When I echo you, I don't disinherit my own feelings—no interpretations. To reverse is to do the opposite. What I do may be a betrayal of myself. When you do the opposite, and I try it on, I may discover that betrayal. My laughter turns to your tears and comes home.

I love to talk. I am highly verbal and have a soft, well-modulated voice. I am not allowed to talk. If I speak at all, it must be gibberish. My actions have to match what I say in gibberish. I start my usual windmilling arm movement. I am warding off blows to my head. I cover my eyes and ears. You mirror what I do. I don't like what I see. You echo it and metamorphose my windmilling into stabs. I stab with my arms; I stab with my feet, my pelvis. More free. I am swinging haymakers. I am fucking angry. I don't like you and swing closer to you. I pummel and cower. I kick back and forth, striking out with pointed finger. You don't want my body. I berate you. I push you around, force you into a corner . . . Minutes . . . I reverse into giggling sensuality. Our bodies intertwining and writhing. Oh, the touch of you!

Opening: I am rolling on the floor. Breath is hard to come by. I mutter incoherently and in rhyme. I do verbal fantasy flights while crashing into walls. My eyes bug; my tongue sticks out. I am alternately totally rigid, totally flaccid. My eyes roll; I sputter, gag and dry-heave. I see the clock hand move through twenty minutes. It takes me twenty minutes to accept a proffered hand. The group holds me in their arms, rocking me gently while humming. Thank God, I'm home at last. I'm safe again, at last. I just can't reach out. I fear never getting out of one of these spells. The group lifts me to arms' length overhead and carries me. I am resurrected but totally limp in their hands. . . . I'm safe.

Wallowing: I am hanging on to a pillow, being dragged around the room. My eyes are closed. I am yelling for Mommy. There are no other words. I keep my eyes closed in embarrassment and shame. I am jerked around the room hanging on to the pillow. I will not let go.

Longing: The room is darkened. I hold him, rocking and crooning a lullaby. He abruptly pulls away from me. I reach out my arms and coax him to come back. He doesn't. I stretch my arms farther and farther. My eyes are closed. My arms ache. Suddenly, I am calling, "Mommy! Mommy!" My arms are railroad tracks going over the horizon.

Forcing: I love the whole world. I walk with my arms stretched out wide to everyone. I am beautiful and at ease. We should all love each other. No one comes to meet me. I reach out but no one reaches back. I feel ignored. Why do you walk around with your eyes covered? Others walk away. Some cross their arms and just stare at me. Look at me! Look at me! Stretch your arms out to me, you bastard! You look over my head. You look at my feet. You look everywhere except at my eyes.

Losing: I can't reach out. My hands are behind my back. I am struggling to bring them forward. I try to stretch out my hands toward the group. I prevent myself all the time. Ican'tIcan'tIwon'tIwon't. . . . I'm afraid. . . . I'm afraid. I am a record on automatic replay. I must be exhausted and worn with wearing to be lying on the floor calling out, "Help me! Help me!"

Changing: I scream at a hundred decibels. I sit and rock and hold my ears and scream and scream. The sound comes from way down and from far away. I hurt so. I don't show that things affect me. I love that long wail. It shivers my spine and hollows my head. It is pure. It's been a long time since I've been pure.

Dr. Laura Perls

Notes on the Psychology of Give and Take

"It's give and take." This most felicitous English phrase (no other language has its equal) indicates the very essence of relationship. "To give" and "to take" are not merely transitive verbs in the narrow grammatical sense. They imply as objects not only what is given or taken, but the act of giving and the act of taking, both having each other as objects. Between them they comprise the whole range of the social process, the aim of which is the balance of the social field, while growth continues.

The alert, ongoing, ever-changing awareness of the plus and minus in the social situation we call Justice. Justice is blind; for the eye—according to the figure-ground information—is the organ of preference. The kinesthetic sense is the organ of balance, so Justice is pictured holding a pair of scales; and to balance them, "it's give and take."

Spontaneous Give and Take

The PRESENT is something that just "is," held out, offered.

The German word for a present is *"Geschenk."* *"Schenken"* means "pouring out"; *"der Schenke"* is the man who pours wine at table (Songs of Hafiz, West-Oestl. Divan, etc.); *"die Schenke"* or *"der Ausschank"* means "the inn." *Geschenk* is thus something poured out, overflowing, obtained without effort. It comes from abundance (cornucopia, Mother Earth, Land of Milk and Honey, etc.).

The present is not a sacrifice, but something that is given easily and without expectations on the side of the giver. It is also not a surprise or reward, but what is naturally expected and looked for in an established community, as the baby expects the mother's milk. For the infant everything is (or should be) *Geschenk,* the natural, easy fulfillment of natural desire.

The infant is not (and need not be) grateful. Gratitude is the response to the unexpected gift, to the undeserved benefit, in short, to an act of grace. One feels grateful for the release from guilt feelings, for the reestablishment of the feeling of belonging. One does not feel and express special gratitude for what is coming to him in the natural course of events, within which it is as compelling for the mother to give as it is for the child to receive nourishment.

The present restores the integrity of the giver as well as of the receiver. The free correspondence between abundance and need guarantees the balance of the social field.

Christmas Old-Style

The original oral significance of the present is very obviously expressed in the European Christmas customs. Santa Claus comes with a big sack chock full of nuts, fruit, and candy which he empties in the middle of the room, and all the kids grab as much as they can hold. In Germany the *pièce de résistance* of every individual heap of Christmas presents is a plateful of the traditional Christmas cookies, nuts, raisins, fruit, candy, etc. Prior to the industrial manufacture of Christmas decorations the main decorations of the Christmas tree, apart from the candles, were edible. The tree, studded with lights and laden with food in the middle of winter, is a happy manifestation of man's sense of abundance and justice, symbolizing the effort to compensate for the darkness and barrenness of nature.

Presents were given mainly to children and other dependents, to the poor, etc.

The main event of Christmas Day was the big meal, the feeding of servants, employees, orphans, paupers, etc. Grown-ups in the same social or economic category did not give each other presents, as that would have meant imposing and incurring obligations, which would run contrary to the true spirit of *Schenken*. And certainly no dependent was expected to put himself to any expense for a present to anyone better off than himself, *i.e.*, to make a sacrifice. The needy had a natural right to the present, without obligation, without "deserving," etc.

The same attitude is reflected in the custom of giving birthday presents. For your birthday you get something not even because you are needy—let alone "deserving" —but simply because you "are." With the recognition of your existence as a human being, your potential neediness is taken for granted. The world is a present for every human child; the good and bad fairies or the Three Wise Men are present at every birth. Adults, who all the year round deprive children of their birthright, atone by giving Christmas and birthday presents.

Christmas New-Style

Atonement is not an act of justice; it is not based on the acute and responsible awareness of actual need. It stems from the vague sense of obligation which, in the complicated structure of our society, is replacing more and more the spontaneous and discriminating awareness of relationship. Nowadays the Christmas or birthday present makes up not so much for the need of the receiver as for the guilt feelings of the giver. Thus, it does not restore the balance of the social field, but creates additional unbalance through disappointment on the side of the receiver and resentment on the side of the giver, who—in order to alleviate his guilt feelings and to produce a semblance of social balance—has to invest the Christmas gift with a significance far beyond its actual value. He becomes an advertising agent who has to convince the receiver that he really needs and wants what he is getting. As little as possible is spent on gifts that are made to look worth a million. "Good will to men" becomes something printed smaller and smaller on more and more artistic Christmas cards and packed—in niggardly amounts and inferior quality—in more and more ingenious wrappings.

The sense of obligation is the vague acceptance of social involvement without the acute awareness that would make the discharge of obligation a limited and socially valid act. Discharge of obligation does not release giver and receiver into a more balanced relationship, but creates a new bond—as the name indicates—of unlimited mutual obligation. Thus, it introduces the whole vicious circle of competition and bribery, futile sacrifice, disappointment, resentment, and guilt.

The annual Christmas farce leaves everybody exhausted physically, emotionally, financially; in January we are sick, mean, and broke. From a symbol of man's love and justice, Christmas has degenerated into a racket, the very characteristic of which is that it throws the social process out of balance.

As in our urbanized and industrialized civilization it has become increasingly difficult and in fact impossible to be fully aware of the social situation and one's place in it, many previously effective social attitudes (measures to restore balance in the social field) have become distorted and invalid.

Creative and Injurious Sacrifice

Making a SACRIFICE originally implies the giving up of something of lesser for something of greater value. It breaks up the wholeness of personal integrity in order to achieve integrity on a superpersonal level. As the word "sacrifice" indicates, it has mainly a religious (or social, which is originally the same) significance. It means making oneself whole through communion with the Divine, giving up the pleasures on earth for the life hereafter; sacrificing one's sexuality for the love of Christ or one's private life for the good of the community.

The sacrifice would place an enormous responsibility on the receiver, if it were not that in the religious or social context the sacrificer makes himself responsible (by prayer and meditation and social activity), so his sacrifice will not be in vain. He need not burden God or society with guilt feelings even for his non-achievement, for by his very sacrifice he is absolved from his own guilt feelings. Thus the sacrifice, however great, never amounts to a real deprivation, but to an intrapersonal restructuring of the personality, away from more personal and along more impersonal lines.

In interpersonal relationships, on the other hand, the sacrifice amounts practically to a bribe. A strong love or family relationship may be a borderline case (the sexual context, too, is im-personal), but any interpersonal contact tends to place all responsibility for the sacrifice of something lesser for something greater on the receiver. The sacrificer expects the receiver to grow on his sacrifice, *i.e.*, to show and appreciate his (the receiver's) gain, which alone would make the sacrifice worthwhile. The interpersonal sacrifice tries to elicit from the receiver something (love, affection, recognition, gratitude, etc.) that otherwise might not be forthcoming. The sacrificer lacks self-esteem and tries to force it from the receiver, *i.e.*, he inflates whatever he is giving or doing, he "rubs it in," so that the receiver should not for a moment forget it. As he has projected his own unrealized need for wholeness on the receiver, the sacrificer can never do enough and can never get enough. He continually tries to escape his own guilt feelings by throwing them on the receiver.

While the genuine superpersonal sacrifice gives up something of definitely appreciated personal value for the union with something greater, the interpersonal sacrifice buys personal appreciation and thus compensates for the lack of self-esteem. Disappointment is inevitable, for the more that is given, the more that is taken for granted by the receiver, so that less and less appreciation is forthcoming, while the sacrificer gets progressively more and more impoverished and disintegrated.

While the interpersonal sacrifice is usually made by immature and insecure people, the genuine (superpersonal) sacrifice is an act of maturity and insight. The Buddha gives up a life of pleasure and dissipation for the way of poverty and concentration at the age of forty. Christ walks to the Cross at the age of thirty-three. Abraham prepares to sacrifice Isaac, whom he has begotten in his old age, and only at the last moment is he blessed by the insight that his own personal sacrifice of the apple of his eye is as nothing compared with the promise of future generations upon generations living in the sight of the Lord. To resign the sacrifice, and with it one's own immediate intrapersonal integration, is perhaps the greatest sacrifice—so great, indeed, that Abraham in his senility (or childishness) is not quite able to carry it off. The slaughtering of the ram in place of the original sacrifice again amounts to a bribe. It is a childish dummy device, a substitute that makes it possible to externalize one's guilt feelings (the evidence of lack of integration) and thus efficiently to prevent any intrapersonal or intra-group reorganization. The difference between the scape-goat and the golden calf is, after all, not so very great!

Bribery and Blackmail

The BRIBE is an a priori payment for a not yet committed betrayal. In order to be successful, the bribe has to be attractive enough, *i.e.*, of sufficient material or social advantage to the receiver to tempt him to make a switch in moral allegiance. It must be strong enough to break a previous commitment and to overcome the guilt feelings connected with such a break by forming a more promising bond of loyalty.

Only the dissatisfied and frustrated are open to bribery; only the greedy and insatiable are prone to pay bribes. It is, in fact, the same type of person who—depending on actual circumstances—either pays or takes bribes. It is the infantile, insecure hanger-on, who does not feel convinced of the legitimacy of his own needs and demands and who has no confidence in his ability to command consideration and respect.

Both the giver and receiver of a bribe are open to BLACKMAIL and are potential blackmailers. They have to take good care of each other: the briber's generosity must never flag; the bribed one's subservience must be perpetually assured. As the briber and the bribed feel equally guilty, they feel equally threatened by exposure. And blackmail is nothing else but extortion (of money or other advantages), by the threat of exposure.

Of course, bribery is not an indispensable condition for blackmail. Indeed, any knowledge about anything that could potentially discredit anyone in the eyes of anyone else can be used for the purpose of extortion. Where, as in a totalitarian society, the disintegration of individual human relationships becomes a political goal, bribery and blackmail become the foremost political devices.

But we have learned from experience in our own time that no balanced society can be established by methods that are liable to increase the guilt feelings and to produce the mutual contempt of its members. The degree of callousness and brazenness necessary to get rid of the ensuing depression sets in motion the whole paranoiac process of desensitization and projection, suspicion, feeling attacked and persecuted, looking for scapegoats, attack and destruction, and finally self-destruction.

NOTES ON THE PSYCHOLOGY OF GIVE AND TAKE

Payment and Reward

One should expect that the most successful way of balancing the social process would be an exact exchange of values. But unfortunately, "an eye for an eye and a tooth for a tooth" applies only in the field of retribution and punishment. Since it first was refuted by the Wisdom of Solomon, much ink has flowed already to prove the invalidity of this primitive principle, which presupposes an undeveloped, undifferentiated sense of values, *i.e.*, an unawareness of the necessities and possibilities in the actual situation.

We shall confine ourselves here to a discussion of two other aspects of value exchange, namely, PAYMENT and REWARD.

Payment is made as a monetary or material equivalent either for goods or for work. It is given in recognition of value, which in turn is defined by temporary economic circumstances, depending on supply and demand.

Reward, on the other hand, is an expression of appreciation of merit. Any meritorious action stands alone, "on its own merit." There are no comparable standards of value that could be adequately expressed in money. Thus, a reward may consist of a sum of money (which then is quite arbitrarily decided on), but it may also consist of a medal or a diploma or a title, or the recognition and gratitude of one's fellow men, or simply in the consciousness of a thing well done.

Promotion in military or civil service is partly a reward, an appreciation of merit. But as far as it is expected with regularity and connected with continuing material advantages it is payment for service.

The American or European physician is paid for services rendered on a generally accepted scale, so and so much per visit or operation or psychotherapeutic session. The Chinese physician is paid when his cure has been successful, *i.e.*, he is rewarded for a unique effort.

In a general way one could say that the more meritorious the effort—*i.e.*, the more it contributes to a genuine social balance—the less it is rewardable in money. Thus, the police reward, which is promised and given for information, is simply payment for betrayal, which falls more under the category of "bribery" than "reward." On the other hand, "virtue is its own reward." The most incessant and selfless services and sacrifices remain not only unpaid and unrewarded, but must be taken for granted. Only the limited work or object can be paid for with a limited amount of money; only the limited service or effort can be rewarded with promotion or a title or a citation. The unlimited devotion of a parent or the lifelong dedication to a cause cannot be paid for or rewarded, it can only be accepted and need not even be recognized. Its reward is in the actual performance, in the feeling of restoring the social balance in a changing ongoing process.

Paul Goodman

Golden Age

1. *Freud and the Egyptians*

The murder of the father of the primal horde, the angry aspect of the Oedipus complex—for Freud this is the beginning of history, and he finds everywhere that history and culture is the reactive response to it. Nevertheless, there is never absent, in his thinking, the inkling of an "earlier amiable" condition, "the only satisfactory relationship," as he says, that between the mother and her infant son. In mythology this condition is the Saturnian or Golden Age, a miraculous era of fulfillments, without scarcities or jealousies. But though Freud has much to say about the later mischances of the Saturnian race, the cannibalism and the emasculation, he does not tend to expatiate on the Saturnian peace. It is said,

Happy is the people that has no history—where there are only finished situations as the seasons roll—and, conversely, there is no use of writing a history of happiness. Why *write* it?

Another example of Freud's avoidance of the deeper dream is his coolness to the theories and the occasional evidences of a primitive matriarchy. What a curious thing that Freud, of all people, should mention so rarely the ideas of Bachofen and the others! And when he does mention them, he derives the matriarchy, as a reaction, from the murderous sons' renunciation of the murdered father's women: presumably, these older women are identified with the dead man and are forbidden. But surely it is not farfetched to think of the matriarchy as repeating also the primitive infantile joy.

I should like to suggest, however, that the strange speculation of Freud's last years, whereby Moses is made an Egyptian, is a more positive reference to the Golden Age of love. A hundred critics have explained that in this speculation, making Moses a "gentile," Freud at last takes vengeance on the Jews, on his father's religion so burdensome to himself. But this is superficial, for Freud does not make Moses a "gentile" at all, in the sense of a Christian gentile whose lineage he derives precisely as a reaction to the Jews. (His "vengeance" turns quite the other way.) Freud makes Moses not a gentile but an Egyptian, of the house of the Pharaohs. And what is this house? Its most salient characteristic is that it is the royal incestuous family, and therefore divine. It is the house of the descendants of the wedded brother and sister. Elsewhere Freud speaks of "the most maiming wound" inflicted on mankind by civilization, the ban against incest; but the Pharaohs did not suffer so severely from this wound as the rest of mankind. (And, of course, "royal" and "incestuous" are equated not only in Egypt.)

We must therefore conceive of the Freudian anthropology somewhat as follows: first the Egyptians, of divine lineage, civilized and sessile; then the wandering primal horde led by Moses; then the remorseful father-murderers, the Jews, reactively righteous in the Law; and then the Christians, rebeling against the constraints of righteousness. Add on to this the latest generation, the neurotics, and we have a respectable modern theogeny.

Why was Freud reluctant to explore the earlier, less gloomy condition, dwelling only on the frustration and the murder? This is usually, and truly enough, attributed to his own character and behavior: he was paternal, filially rebellious, stern, self-denying, law-abiding, the "father of the psychoanalytic movement"; or, at a more impersonal remove, he was the conscientious voice of objective science (which he took to be "reality"), the rebel against established convention, banded with his brotherly co workers, etc., etc. Finally, however, I think a more material, and *therefore* more ennobling, explanation can be given by Reich's conception of "primary masochism": the tension of unfinished love tries to burst asunder the inner constraints to its fulfillment, and this is felt by the subject as a longing to be burst, punctured, injured, destroyed. The earlier dream is too anxious-making and dangerous to dwell with. The closer one comes to orgasm without giving in to it, and so it happens in "successful" classical psychoanalysis, the more violent become the sadomasochistic dreams of fire, slaughter, and cosmic explosion. Now in both himself and the patients he treated most successfully, Freud came to this deep place and saw these terrible things; he could not, or dared not, by his techniques, break through. Naturally, then, he was obliged as a good and honest observer to say that the deeper you went, the more apparently you wanted to die.

Freud speculates in the grand philosophical style; he is free and easy with the theoretical formulations (for what difference does it make? theory is made for man, not man for theory), but in his context, and recurrent reference, he is always square in the center of present, obvious, and important experience, of his own behavior, his patients' dreams, the laws of the state. He dreams the sadomasochistic wish, fire and revolution in the social order, *and still the constraint and the self-constraint hold firm;* you can twist it and turn it any way you want, but this is history, biography, and autobiography. This is what he is telling us in the famous chapter beginning, "Let us now envisage the scene of such a totemic meal." The plot is a fiction, but there is not a significant detail that is not obligated by what he found in himself, his healthiest patients' deepest dreams, and the mores of society.

When he became very old, on the other hand (the tension of longing less, and the need to rally less—and this is interpreted by the subject as "now I am succeeding in dying"), he dreamed a more inclusive dream and conceived of Freud-Moses as an Egyptian of the House of Pharaoh.

2. Seven Ways of Coping with the Fact that We Do Not Live in the Golden Age

I

The first way is to deny that it is a fact, to forget that there was a terrible incident, and to go on. This method is so commonplace, it is almost our political constitution, that we have to remind ourselves how remarkable it is. It is alternately expressed by saying, There is no Golden Age (it is utopian) or We live in a Golden Age. Forgetful, with varying degrees of conviction we rush or falter into one another's embrace.

It does not work out very well, for what is forgotten comes, precisely, to be remembered. The question is how it can work out at all. Let us again recall the story of Oedipus and Jocasta who embraced in willful forgetfulness (Speaking of Sophocles' play, Aristotle calls their ignorance an "improbability outside the plot"; but Sophocles, of course, has made their willful ignorance just the essence of the motivation.) Jocasta slays herself and Oedipus blinds himself. Let us say that Jocasta slays herself in order to be again with Laius, whom she loves, for her pleasure with Oedipus has revived a deeper longing; she has come to mourn for the first time. And that Oedipus blinds himself in order not to look on with frustrated envy. *This* is the state in which we live and cope with

the fact that we do not live in the Golden Age: somewhere there is an entranced fixation on a past happiness—
not ours; and we flounder in darkness in order not to
suffer intolerable envy.

II

Suppose, on the contrary, we proceed in full consciousness and have a society that is workaday and efficient like some of the primitives they write about.
Certain compromises and drawings-of-the-line are necessary, perhaps most especially in the niceties of eating.

The mothers have diminished their loss by taking the
place of rule. The men assume the old prerogatives and
exercise their sexual prowess. By these compromises
much damage of the past is undone. We are in the
Golden Age; and also, in this daylight economy, it is as
if the Golden Age had never been.

Nevertheless the feast must be periodically renewed
in order to prevent forgetting and relapsing into the bad
night of Oedipus. Our activities conform to etiquette
and are circumscribed by taboos. Especially, I say, what
concerns eating, eating something up, is limited by niceties and restrictions. And there are taboos about the
mothers: for none of us must be allowed to loom in the
age of omnipotence, since then once again father would
exist, and the many fathers, grown equally strong, would
tear one another limb from limb. But the mothers say:
"Live at peace, love one another. If you embraced us,
you would revive ancient delusions and it would be the
end of us all. You may embrace, freely, anybody in the

other line." It is sad for them not to have their own men around.

Our constitution is a game. The rules are devised to permit, to excite, the maximum of spontaneity, the most violent exercise possible without destroying the game. Also the rules are really changeable by us, but of course they are sacred and one pretends that they are not being changed. We play our game with serious joy and our etiquette is more important to us than morals.

III

Some of us do not deny the fact, but we defy it. We will not draw any lines, and our games heighten into brawls. We live in the Cities of the Plain and take our pleasures variously and strike and kill.

We carry on in the face of the image of the Golden Age. Every gratification is ritually lawless, it is obligatorily unnatural, counter to what would come to be by growth. Obviously, as is told in the history of our cities, it is the angels who are most sought for, to debauch and kill; the daughters of Lot are not equally desirable. Each bout of love ending in murder blacks out the nagging past.

Contrary to what you imagine, our state of indiscriminate rapine is not impermanent, for it is intermitted by satiation and fatigue. Just because the ritual demands that every possibility be experimented to the extreme, our strength fails in good time and we faint away. We awaken again to desire.

Our fear—for unfortunately we are afraid, otherwise

all would be well—is lest desire itself fail, the penis not be erect, the vagina frigid. We feel called on to bring it to the test, and so we anticipate the need; we suffer a stirring of desire before we are in the presence of any-thing desirable, and the sweat of effort stands on our brows.

But at least this hot, fitful dream is better than the clear daylight of the goodies.

IV

Disgusted with it. On the first day ignorant; on the second hemmed round by rules and careful not to over-step the line; on the third striving to the extreme, and finding that we fail. Rather finally accept the punish-ment and atone, and be received back into the Golden Age. The Great Mother says, "Give it up! give it up! We cannot have it as men used to. He stands there in your experience and mine, lifting his monstrous right. My children, I also feared and hated that Golden Age, as now it seems when I am deprived—for thinking back at joy, it seems to have been pain.

"Take a stone knife. Castrate yourselves. And then we shall live innocently together. Are we not again mother and infant, as in the Golden Age?"

We who have castrated ourselves constitute the priestly rule. We are by no means deprived of all pleas-ure; usually we eat well and are fat as pigs. We are pathically cleanly. Our rule is strict and cruel and gives us plenty of satisfaction. The taxes are high.

Yet there is no bloodshed or rebellion. Those who

136

submit console themselves with the beautiful thought that we fathers are castrated. We who rule resent everything whatever and give plenty of cause for resentment. In place of the dead weight of guilt and loss, there is the continual friction of active resentment. This realm of universal love is very like the Golden Age.

The Great Mother smiles on her priests. It is not the case that she smiles equally on the others. From time to time she is given to fits of unpredictable cruelty that sadden one and all alike.

v

Some of us, entrenched in academies, have elaborated the following Herodian conspiracy, saying: "Look, these young ones are again growing in strength and menace. Even now, just by existing and changing, they are forcing us into old age and death; by living, they force us out of life. Therefore, let us be prudent and slay them while they are small and weak. In this way we can arrest the flight of time and be safe."

The inquisition of the elders is continuous and subtle. In order to survive, it is necessary for the young to be born with the physiognomy of the aged. This is difficult but not impossible, and these communities based on infanticide have also proved viable.

For instance, there is a king who tells himself that he is young in spirit and he loves to surround himself with the fresh faces and the spontaneous gestures and thoughts of children. He sends out his messengers and he fills his court with pretty girls and boys, and he takes pleasure in their sports. And these children, miraculously, do not change; they never, by growing up, remind the king that he is year by year older and is already an old man. For every year all the children are snatched away and destroyed and replaced by other, identical children a year younger. It is easy to find other, identical children; really all children are alike. So this king and his court live in the Golden Age.

So we teachers in universities do not grow old; we are young in spirit. But I, unfortunately, have found that after two or three years of it I have grown bored and prematurely old; for the new kids make the very same errors and it is I who have changed and cannot rally to the task again and again.

VI

But whatever else we do (and some do one thing and some another), all of us repeat the heroic act by which Aeneas founded Rome. Fleeing from his burning homeland, Aeneas lifted his father Anchises from the ground and carried him on his shoulders.

At first he rode on our shoulders, like a burdensome old man of the sea. But we have learned, like Aeneas, to project him further, to throw him high into the sky. And when he rides the sky, he scarcely intervenes in our affairs.

This is the state that we presently see about us in America. He has become the rational truth in which we all believe; the truth does not intervene in our desires or in our wars: we take them where we wish, no fear. We understand them through and through. For us nothing is fearsome or guilty or at a loss, for we know what it is, and we say, "Aha! it is only this—"

It is *only* this: We live by the constitution that all things, and we are among the things, are knowable; we have displaced upward our Golden Age. It does not intervene in our needs; the truth has nothing to do with our needs.

Sometimes we explain it this way: there is an Objective World. This is a convenient formulation, for by becoming aware of every detail of this objective world (and we have techniques for becoming aware of any detail you wish), we can circumvent the awakening in us of any concern. We are not afraid, we are not at a loss, we do not mourn, but we say, "It is (only) this." For there is an objective world, and what has that got to do with me?

Given this wonderful freedom, it is possible by new knowledge, safeguarded by more and more alienating intermediaries, to approximate as closely as we wish the Golden Age.

The danger—but it is a small one—is that someone in an unguarded moment may directly touch on something real and be lost in love and anger.

VII

We do miracles. These are deeds that are in the nature of things growing into the next moment. They are matters of fact. In the situation in which there has been a terrible incident, and we do not live in the Golden Age, such matters of fact are called miracles.

For we are blind—then to do a matter of fact is a miracle. Or there are ritual rules—then to do a matter of fact is a miracle. Or we anticipate desire—then to do a matter of fact is a miracle. We are impotent—then to do a matter of fact is a miracle. Or the dead past has us in grip—then to do a matter of fact is a miracle. Or there is an objective world—then to do a matter of fact is a miracle.

Yet it *is* dark, there *is* an objective world, etc.; and nevertheless there continually come to be matters of fact.

It is as if a man should screw up his courage, close his eyes, take a deep breath, murmur a prayer—for a fearful dive into the abyss—and then proceed, with open eyes, breathing normally and humming a song, a next step on what is tolerably familiar ground.

In times of terrible violence, as in the woods at the end of March, there is a swelling and cracking—I have been disgusted and horrified at it; but afterward one does think of those images as images of danger.

It is not that we do *not* live in the Golden Age and do not have to cope with that fact. On the contrary, who would dare to deny it—today! as the case is!—that a dead man is lying there? The miracle workers do not disregard it but wail loudly; they beat themselves and tear their flesh and mix blood and tears and cry out: "Father! father! except for us the thread of the generations would be cut short."

This is a matter of fact. Except for us the thread of the generations *would* be cut short—as the lad said after

he had done in papa and mama with his new home-
made shotgun.

3. *On the Question: "How Did We Lapse?"*

How did man first lapse from the Saturnian Age in
which we were engaged and happy as one could be as
a matter of fact—just how much that is, is a matter of
fact; how did we lapse from it into the misery of resig-
nation and being beaten and browbeaten? When we
consider the many clever and arduous expedients that
we are capable of, the puzzle presents itself how we are
so wretched.

It is a classical question, and several different explanations are given. These explanations are not unsatisfactory
and, especially if they are considered as operating dy-
namically together so that they heighten one another,
they seem to add up to a sufficient reason. What is interesting about them, however, is that all of them imply an
accident somewhere along the line; and this is unsatisfactory, for our misery seems so ingrained that it calls
for an explanation from our essential natures.

It is likely, for instance, that because of some climatic
or geological catastrophe, men were temporarily deprived of matter-of-fact necessities. They would then
suffer from primary anxiety. In order to feel something
again, they would, like primary masochists, seek out those
who would punish and subdue them, perhaps provoking
to it those innocent of any such need.

Or conversely—this is the usual theory of the foundation of states—a small violent and sadistic group might descend on an aboriginal population, rape its women and its wealth, and subjugate the majority to perpetuate its own prerogatives. The innocent victims are unversed in the arts of force and cunning necessary to protect themselves; they fall an easy prey. Now it is not unlikely that there should be such violent bands in the first place, for frustration leads to aggression and there are numerous chances of frustration.

These accidents, moreover, could have occurred so long ago that by the time there was a proper human species at all it could have been already formed to subjugation. Thus, Freud and his authors speak of the Primal Horde as an original property of man: that is, a superego, the tendency to introject a superego, is innate in the species (as Kropotkin had already said that social mutual aid was innate in the species). And this opinion is likely, if we consider that human children are so long weakly and dependent, and learn what they learn by imitation. For children (such is the theory) have boundless desires and think they are omnipotent; they are wrong—their desires go far beyond their powers and they are frustrated; they then identify themselves with what is big and strong and frustrating. This sequence can be seen every day in nurseries, and it is likely that it is the nature of man.

Yet how puzzling, obvious as it seems! For how, by nature, can desire reach beyond power, since desire is adjusting of the state of things, one desires in an environment that is one's own environment? One desires what in a sense one knows, and one knows only what one does; how, then, can one desire what one does not also potentially do? There is, of course, such a thing as experiment or play. Surely it was by some accident that the children came to be "weak" and "dependent," granted that this accident might have occurred before the human species appeared on the scene.

So the various natural theories imply an accident somewhere along the line. As such they are not adequate to our despair. The theologians, however, insist that our misery is essential to us. This is intolerable to our hope. I should like to suggest that, as frequently, the theologians misinterpret the Bible text on which they build.

The Bible explains that it was the knowledge of good and evil that caused our lapse from innocence and, soon, the expulsion from paradise. Now this does not mean knowledge as such, as some have said, for in innocence Adam named the beasts. Nor does it mean the particular knowledge of sexuality, for Adam and Eve must have had sexual intercourse in innocence, although the fact that they "knew that they were naked" was evidence of their guilt. Is, then, as many have said, the fatal knowledge of good and evil to be contrasted with the ignorance of good and evil—to be ignorant is to be innocent? Surely not, for in the garden they knew every good thing and, in the usual commentary, especially of the poets, they praised it as good. The meaning must then be: what was sinful was the *knowledge of good as cut off from other ways of living the good*. They fell from innocence when they knew and judged and did not act and enjoy. (So they knew they were naked and covered themselves rather than doing something else.) This interpretation is given by Kafka:

> We are sinful not merely because we have eaten of the Tree of Knowledge, but also because we have not yet eaten of the Tree of Life. The state in which we find ourselves is sinful quite independent of guilt.

The Biblical story puts us on the track of an answer to our question "How did we lapse?" *That* question, says the Bible, cannot be answered; every explanation must necessarily seem accidental and arbitrary. For by taking thought, one cannot know anything about the Golden Age. It is taking thought itself that restricts us to the conditions of misery. The Golden Age is known only to the happy, and the happy do not devote themselves—how could they?—to the discussion of objective questions. To pose the question as we pose questions, as a problem of truth and evidence, is already to be sunk in the needs and functions of the Base Age. We have a kind of knowledge of the Golden Age, by way of dreams and hopes, but from these one cannot frame a compelling argument.

We see this in every detail of our experience. From our fears, inhibitions, disgusts, and resentments, from our state institutions and social mores, we can argue more or less compellingly to a terrible incident, we froze, we murdered the father of the primal horde, we wear a rigid armor, our children imagine an infinite destruction, etc., etc. From the data of the objective world, external and internal, we can prove hypotheses less and less relevant to our concern in the present moment. These are typical functions of the Base Age. But from our flashes of happiness and our flushes of concern we do not find that, using words in a rational way, we can conclude anything at all. Conversely (what a blessing!) we do not find that by the rational use of words and evidence we can convince a man to fall in love, to feel concern, to be happy or unhappy. Our happiness consists simply in matters of fact, miracles.

"How did we lapse?" is not a meaningful question; but there is a related question that is meaningful: "Under what conditions do men seek to answer the meaningless but necessary and necessarily meaningless question, 'How did we lapse?'?" "What is the meaning of life?" is not a meaningful question; but there is a meaningful related question, "Under what conditions do men ask themselves the question, 'What is the meaning of life?'?" If I had the learning, I should explore these questions. For my own part, this much learning I have; I come to them when, attempting to be quiet and at ease, I consult my memories and my plans instead of giving way to the cries of anger and pain that would otherwise overwhelm me.

A Selected Bibliography
of Books and Articles
Relevant to
Gestalt Theory
COMPILED BY THE EDITOR

BOSS, MEDARD, *Psychoanalysis and Daseinsanalysis*, Ludwig Lefebre, trans. (New York: Basic Books, 1963).

BUBER, MARTIN, *I and Thou* (New York: Scribners, 1958).

——, *Between Man and Man* (London: Kegan Paul, 1947), especially the essay entitled "Dialogue."

GOODMAN, PAUL, *Utopian Essays and Practical Proposals* (New York: Vintage, 1964), especially essays entitled "On a Writer's Block," "Seating Arrangements; An Elementary Lecture in Functional Planning," "Notes on a Remark of Seami," and "Pornography and the Sexual Revolution."

——, *The Empire City* (New York: Macmillan, 1964).

——, *Growing Up Absurd* (New York: Random House, 1960).

——, *Five Years* (New York: Brussel and Brussel, 1966), especially all sections headed "Psychology."

HEIDEGGER, MARTIN, *Being and Time* (London: SCM Press, 1962).

HERRIGEL, EUGEN, *Zen in the Art of Archery* (New York: Pantheon, 1953).

LAING, RONALD D., *The Politics of Experience* (New York: Pantheon, 1967).

LAO-TZU, *The Way of Life*, Witter Bynner, trans. (New York: Capricorn, 1962).

MAY, ROLLO, *et al.*, *Existence, A New Dimension in Psychiatry and Psychology* (New York: Basic Books, 1958).

MORENO, J. L., *Psychodrama*, Vol. I, 3rd edition (Beacon, New York: Beacon House, 1964).

NARANJO, CLAUDIO, *I and Thou: Here and Now; Contributions of Gestalt Therapy* (Big Sur, California: Esalen Institute, 1967).

PERLS, FREDERICK S., HEFFERLINE, RALPH F., and GOODMAN, PAUL, *Gestalt Therapy* (New York: Julian Press, 1951; also published in paperback, New York: Delta Books, 1965).

PERLS, FREDERICK S., *Ego, Hunger and Aggression* (London: George Allen & Unwin, 1947; also in paperback, San Francisco: Orbit Graphic Arts, 1966).

——, "Gestalt Therapy and Human Potentialities," in Herbert A. Otto (ed.), *Explorations in Human Potentialities* (Charles C. Thomas, 1966).

——, "Theory and Technique of Personality Integration," in *American Journal of Psychotherapy*, II, 4, October, 1948.

————, "Workshop vs. Individual Therapy," paper delivered before the American Psychological Association Convention, New York, 1966.

PERLS, LAURA, "The Gestalt Approach," in *Annals of Psychotherapy*, Special Combined Issue, J. Barron and R. A. Harper (eds.), Monograph No. 3 and 4, Vols. 1 and 2, 1961.

REICH, WILHELM, *Character Analysis* (New York: Noonday Press, 1949).

REINHARDT, KURT F., *The Existentialist Revolt* (New York: Frederick Ungar, 1960), especially the "Appendix on Existentialist Psychotherapy."

RUITENBEEK, H.M. (ed.), *Psychoanalysis and Existential Philosophy* (New York: Dutton, 1962), especially "The Theory and Practice of Existential Analysis" by Wilson Van Dusen, "Ontological Insecurity" by Ronald D. Laing, "Existential Psychiatry and Group Psychotherapy" by Thomas Hora.

SMUTS, JAN CHRISTIAN, *Holism and Evolution* (New York: Macmillan, 1926).

WATTS, ALAN, *Psychotherapy, East and West* (New York: Mentor, 1961).

WHYTE, LANCELOT L., *The Next Development in Man* (New York: Mentor, 1950).

RENEWALS: 691-4574

DATE DUE

RENEWALS 691-4574